Euphorbias

Euphorbias

Timothy Walker

CASSELL ILLUSTRATED

THE ROYAL HORTICULTURAL SOCIETY

First published in Great Britain in 2002 by
Cassell Illustrated
Octopus Publishing Group
2–4 Heron Quays, London E14 4PJ

A CIP catalogue record for this book is available
from the British Library
ISBN 0-304-36289-1

Designer: Justin Hunt
Commissioning Editor: Camilla Stoddart

Printed in Slovenia by DELO tiskarna
by arrangement with Prešernova družba

CONTENTS

Title Page:
Euphorbia
characias 'John
Tomlinson' is a
splendid, bold form
of one of the best
euphorbias for all
but the most
exposed gardens. The
flower heads provide
colour for more than
three months.

INTRODUCTION

Euphorbias are an essential component of any garden. They come in an unparalleled range of growth forms, from small annuals to large evergreen shrubs, and they bring a unique colour to containers and borders of all types from early spring to early autumn. There is no garden situation in which at least one euphorbia cannot thrive.

It is an indication of the nebulous nature of the colour of euphorbias that there is no universally accepted word to describe it. Green, yellow-green, yellow, lime-green, acid green and acid yellow have all been used. The best word to collectively describe the colour is 'chartreuse'. Chartreuse is a fiery French liqueur from Grenoble made from herbs and flowers. It is available in bright yellow and bright green varieties and if it is not drunk quickly enough and the unfinished bottle is left in the sun, the green liqueur fades to yellow. In the same way, euphorbias give a range of colours from dark green to bright yellow, although a handful of species and varieties give shades of orange and red for good measure.

Euphorbias have been cultivated as garden plants for at least four centuries and for all of that time they have borne the same vernacular name – spurges. To some people the annual British species, such as *Euphorbia helioscopia* and *E. peplus* (the sun and petty spurges respectively), are meddlesome weeds that get in the way of their intended plantings, but these plants could never be described as pernicious weeds. The best known of all euphorbias is probably poinsettia (*Euphorbia pulcherrima*) which

Euphorbia polychroma is one of the most common spurges in British gardens and one of the best herbaceous perennials. It provides a particularly clean yellow in spring that combines very well with blues and other yellows.

adorns so many European homes at Christmas. This species is a common garden plant in frost-free parts of the world where it makes a good border plant.

The largest genus in the world

There are over 150 species, varieties and cultivars of *Euphorbia* listed in the latest edition of the *RHS Plant Finder* and they are the subject of this handbook. However, these euphorbias are just the tip of the iceberg since at least 2,000 species exist worldwide, with examples on every continent except Antarctica. In fact, *Euphorbia* is the largest genus of plants in the world with only *Astragalus* in the pea family coming close.

Many species of *Euphorbia* do not appear in the *RHS Plant Finder* because they are plants that are not hardy in Britain, and therefore require glasshouse conditions if they are to be cultivated. The species that we can grow in our gardens are almost all from the northern cool-temperate regions and the European Mediterranean region with just a handful from northern Africa and elsewhere. Turkey alone is home to 95 species and Europe has 105 of which 25 species are native to Britain. A cool glasshouse with a minimum temperature of 5°C (41°F) is suitable for growing many additional euphorbias, in particular the species from the Canary Islands.

Gardeners use not only the minority of the world's spurges but also the atypical species. Euphorbias have evolved into a myriad of forms from tiny prostrate annuals to trees. A great number are succulent plants with sharp thorns and no leaves except after rains. Across southern Africa these regularly dominate the vegetation. In tropical East Africa, succulent euphorbias grow to tree-like proportions and are often confused with cacti.

There are a number of easy ways to tell whether a cactus or a succulent *Euphorbia* confronts you in the wild. The first step is to look at your map; if you are in Africa, it is a *Euphorbia* but if you are in America, it must be a cactus. The next step is to count the spines; if the spines are in pairs, it is a *Euphorbia* but if the spines are in groups of 5, 6 or more, then it is a cactus. The final test is to scratch the surface of the stem carefully; if a

white, sticky sap oozes from the wound, then the plant is a *Euphorbia* but if the liquid coming from the wound is clear, then the plant is a cactus. You must always remember that other groups of plants, such as members of the periwinkle family, also have white sap. The presence of sap does not prove that a plant is a *Euphorbia* but the absence of sap does prove that a plant is not a member of the genus.

The similarity of the African euphorbias and the American cacti is a good example of convergent evolution. Both of these are plants that have evolved to survive in a hot environment where the meagre rainfall is highly seasonal. A year's supply of rain may fall in just a few weeks. In these circumstances a plant may evolve an efficient rain-collection system in the form of widespread, shallow roots and a rain-storage system, such as a swollen stem. During dry periods, these plants may throw off all their leaves to reduce water loss and all the photosynthesis takes place in cells in the outer layers of the stem.

The flowers and fruits

When plants are grouped and classified, plant taxonomists examine as many features of the plant as possible and compare them with the same features on other plants. Individual plants that share a number of characteristics are then grouped together in the same species. Similar species are grouped into a genus and genera into families. Some plant features are given more importance than others and the appearance of flowers and fruits are top of the list. The 2,000 species of *Euphorbia* share a collection of flower and fruit characteristics found in no other group of plants and it is these characteristics that unify all the plants in this genus. Once you understand the flower structure and combine these observations with other visible characteristics like height and growth habit, all euphorbias can be identified to species level with nothing more sophisticated than a hand lens.

When looking at *Euphorbia* flowers for the first time, put all thought of bright and blowsy sepals or petals such as those found on common garden plants like hellebores, clematis, tulips and geraniums, out of your mind. *Euphorbia* flowers do not indulge in such exhibitionism and have no sepals or petals. If there is a colourful structure near the flowers then it is a leaf which is sometimes referred to as a bract.

The flowers are nearly always borne at the top of the plant at the end of the current year's growth. Near the top of each stem there is normally a ring, or whorl, of leaves looking a bit like a ruff around the neck of an Elizabethan nobleman. Above this ring of leaves are the flowers, although sometimes small shoots of flowers grow from the axils of the upper stem leaves. The flowers are held on a branching structure. This often starts with five branches, each of which then branches into three and each of these then branches into two. The final branches may then divide a further three times. However, this is by no means the only branching pattern and in some cases it is diagnostic for a certain species or group of species. In the 'Species and Cultivated Euphorbias' chapter (see pp.46–89) the branching pattern will be used to help you to identify some of the species in your garden.

Start by examining flowers at the top of the flowerhead. You should see a pair of leaves and within these is a cup-like structure known as a cyathium (plural, cyathia), derived from the

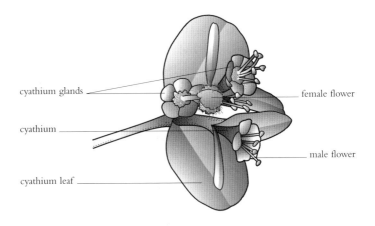

cyathium glands — female flower

cyathium —

— male flower

cyathium leaf —

Greek word for a cup or ladle. These leaves are referred to as the 'cyathium leaves' to distinguish them from the 'stem leaves' and the leaves in the ruff at the bottom of the flowerhead that are sometimes called the 'ray leaves'. The cyathium leaves are normally separate from each other but in a few species, such as *Euphorbia characias*, these are fused together into a saucer-like structure. In a few other species, they are either absent or very small. The stem leaves are normally much longer than they are wide and are often a very different shape from the roundish cyathium leaves. As the flowerhead matures through summer the cyathium leaves often drop off. The illustrations should help you visualise the anatomy of a typical *Euphorbia* flower which will become much clearer as you examine more plants.

Once you have found a cyathium, there should be a ring of swollen appendages around its rim. These are glands that secrete nectar which attracts and rewards pollinators. The more common pollinators are flies, bees, wasps, hoverflies and ants but almost any visiting animal can transport the pollen away to another flower providing pollen is being released at the time of the visit. Ants are particularly common on the flowerheads of the honey-scented *Euphorbia mellifera*. In this instance, the ants aggressively defend their nectar supplies from any incoming animals. Birds are less common as pollinators but bright red cyathium or upper stem leaves usually attract them. Poinsettias *(E. pulcherrima)* are pollinated by birds for example. In windswept environments, where flying insects are rare, snails may be frequent visitors to the nectar glands.

The nectar glands vary in number, colour and shape between species but it is an almost universal truth that within a species the number, shape and colour of the nectar glands is constant. The only common exception to this rule is *Euphorbia characias*, where the glands can vary from round and black through to yellow and crescent-shaped with every possible intermediate state. The glands may have horns or warts attached to them or they may have a totally smooth margin. When the cyathium is young and fresh there may be silky hairs between the glands that can extend right across the mouth of the cyathium. As the growing season progresses, these silky hairs may wither away.

In order to understand the structure of any flowers it is important to remember that their purpose is to facilitate the production of seeds by sexual reproduction. In order to achieve this, flowers produce pollen from the male parts of the flowers, known as stamens. Each stamen consists of a stalk (or filament) and on the end of this is the anther which splits open to release its pollen. During pollination the pollen is taken by the pollinator and transferred to the female part of the flower known as the carpel. The pollen is deposited on the receiving surface of the carpel (the stigma) and here the pollen grain germinates and grows down a tube (the style) towards the ovary which contains the egg. If all goes well, the pollen grain fertilizes the egg to give rise to the embryo that will be included in the seed.

On euphorbias the flowers grow up from inside the cyathium. In the majority of euphorbias the anther consists of two parts and the stamen is T-shaped as a result. The pollen is normally yellow and the outside of the anther may be burgundy-red. As soon as the pollen is shed, the stamens drop off so you will not find them in every cyathium that you look at. Stamens are rarely used to identify species. All *Euphorbia* flowers bear three carpels that are fused together to give one style which branches into three near the top. The end of each branch of the style then splits into two and at the tip of each is a shiny, swollen tip – the surface of the stigma. After fertilization, the fused carpels give rise to a three-seeded capsule that is very characteristic of euphorbias. Along with the colour and shape of the nectar glands, the surface of the seed capsule

The nectar glands of Euphorbia characacias *vary from this black form to plants with crescent-shaped, yellow glands with horns.*

is another very useful feature for identifying individual species since it may be smooth or rough. Furthermore, the seed capsule may be rough just on the crests of each lobe or rough all over, or it may be warty or have sausage-like protrusions, or it may have a deep groove cut in each lobe, or have wings.

When the seed capsules dry, they explode and the mature seeds are expelled. On a sunny day, the fruit of species like *Euphorbia characacias* and *E. lathyris* explode with an easily audible crack. It is possible to use the seed to help separate individual species but in a garden it is often difficult to collect the seed in good condition, so they are not used in this book to identify euphorbias. The seeds often have an oil-rich protuberance known as a caruncle attached to them and this is believed to be involved in the dispersal of the seeds, usually by ants and birds.

The cyathium may appear to be the fused petals of one flower containing the stamens and carpels but this is not true because the cyathium is not homologous with the petals of other flowers. The cyathium is a distinct structure not found in plants of other genera. Each stamen is actually a very simple male flower with neither sepals nor petals; it consists of just one stamen. When the stamen drops off after releasing its pollen, a stump can be seen inside the cyathium. This is the flower stalk (or pedicel). The female flowers are just as simple consisting of just three fused carpels that produce one seed each. This capsule becomes more obvious after pollination as it grows out of the mouth of the cyathium. If there were any petals, they would be attached either to the top or bottom of the capsule or at the bottom of the stamen – petals are never attached to the bottom of the pedicel. *Euphorbia* flowers are single sexed, therefore, but they are arranged in a pattern very similar to that of the stamens and carpels in a bisexual flower like a tulip. Plants with both

13

male and female single-sexed flowers on the same plant are described as monoecious, which literally means 'one home'. If male and female single-sexed flowers are borne on different plants, the plants are described as dioecious, meaning 'two homes'. Some of the succulent euphorbias are dioecious.

Is this detailed information important? Superficially it is not because the cyathium leaves, the cyathium, the nectar glands and the male and female flowers are functionally analogous to a bisexual flower. If, however, you are trying to classify the plant kingdom in a way that reflects the evolutionary history of life on Earth, it is very important. The cyathia with their simple, single-sexed flowers are unique to euphorbias and so euphorbias are therefore recognized as a natural group with one common ancestor.

Flowering times

December	Early	
January	Mid	Winter
February	Late	
March	Early	
April	Mid	Spring
May	Late	
June	Early	
July	Mid	Summer
August	Late	
September	Early	
October	Mid	Autumn
November	Late	

The stem leaves

The stem leaves of garden euphorbias do not vary greatly in terms of shape or arrangement. They are never lobed or divided and the edges of the leaves are either smooth or slightly serrated. None of the species recommended in this handbook have a distinct stalk (or petiole). In shape, the leaves range from linear (long and narrow with more or less parallel edges) to oblong with slightly curved margins. The leaves are nearly always arranged in spirals or on alternate sides of the stem. It is only in the stems of *Euphorbia lathyris* that the leaves are arranged in opposite pairs and these pairs are arranged at right angles to the last pair. The annual, biennial and herbaceous perennial species are by definition not evergreen but the overwintering biennial-shooted species and the shrubs are evergreen. The colour of the leaves varies from species to species, ranging from dark green or blue-silver with a leathery appearance, to pale green with a soft texture and appearance. The central veins of the leaves of some species are a different colour from the bulk of the leaf. These veins may be white, cream or even pink in the case of *E. sikkimensis*. The lower leaves often drop off during the growing season.

In the 'Species and Cultivated Euphorbias' chapter where the best garden species and varieties are described, the stem leaves are not mentioned unless they are useful identification features or they contribute to the garden appeal of the plant. Euphorbias are rarely grown for their leaves alone although the silver leaves of *Euphorbia myrsinites* and similar species or the dark green leaves of *E. amygdaloides* var. *robbiae* are desirable features when the plants are not in flower.

The sap

It has already been stated that the presence of sap does not prove that a plant is a *Euphorbia* but the absence of sap does prove that a plant is not a *Euphorbia*. The chemistry of the sap is complex and well beyond the scope of this book but gardeners who want to grow euphorbias do need to be aware of any potential hazards presented by the sap.

Ideally, you should never allow the sap of euphorbias to come into contact with any part of your body. Some people's skin reacts to *Euphorbia* sap while other people are superficially unaffected. The reaction can vary from a red angry rash to blistering that can last for a few days. In most cases the reaction is greater if the skin is exposed to direct sunlight and if you do react your skin may become increasingly sensitive. Gloves and long-sleeved clothing are normally adequate protection for the gardener but if you do get the sap on your skin and especially your hands (as you may touch other parts of your body with your hands) you must wash the skin very thoroughly. Never allow the sap to come into contact with your eyes. If this does happen, irrigate the eye with water for 15 minutes and go to hospital. Temporary blindness may result but this does not normally last. There is some evidence that the sap is carcinogenic when combined with other substances.

As with most toxic plants, the sap of euphorbias is exploited for medicinal purposes. In some parts of Britain *Euphorbia lathyris* is known as mole-wort which is sometimes misinterpreted to mean that the sap will keep moles out of the soil in your garden. This vernacular name refers to the use of the sap to burn warts or moles off skin (as described in the *Concise Oxford English Dictionary*, no less). *Euphorbia* sap may be

Euphorbia *species often hybridize, both in their original habitats and in gardens. The handsome leaves of this new hybrid between* Euphorbia stygiana *and* E. mellifera *compliment the flower heads of* Eryngium giganteum.

16

of no use in discouraging garden moles but it is extremely toxic to fish. Just a few drops in an ornamental pond will cause the inhabitants to float to the surface looking slightly aggrieved and very dead. The fish die from lacerated gills and death happens so quickly that the flesh of edible fish is still suitable for human consumption. African fisherman have exploited this toxicity for many years but it is not a sustainable means of harvesting fish because it kills young fish as well as those of oven-ready size.

The sap is equally toxic to freshwater snails and worms. This may seem like an irrelevant fact but in tropical Africa snails are hosts to parasitic worms that cause a great deal of human suffering and sometimes death. Medical research is currently underway to test the sap of a wide variety of species of *Euphorbia* and related genera in the Euphorbiaceae family. It is hoped that the sap of some *Euphorbia* species may have a lower level of toxicity to humans while maintaining the toxicity to the snails and worms. Alternatively, it may be possible to chemically alter the sap with the same result.

Elsewhere the sap of a variety of species is used in many different ways. These range from an anti-tumour drug in China (from *Euphorbia fischeriana*) which has been in use for 2,000 years, to a treatment for bee and scorpion stings in Uganda (from *E. hirta*). In India, the sap of *E. tirucalli* has been used as an ingredient of fireworks for centuries and is now being tested as a renewable source of fuel. *E. antisyphilitica* has been harvested in Mexico for many years and boiled to extract its sap which is then cooled to produce candelilla. This wax is used in polishes, for electric insulation materials (when mixed with rubber), for making gramophone records, waterproofing coats, in candles (when mixed with paraffin) and for waxing lemons so the shelf life of the fruit is extended. Given the toxicity of the sap, this latter practice is worrying.

Perhaps the most bizarre use of the sap is by male African rhinos which are known to rub it on their genitalia prior to finding a mate. In his book, *Flora Britannica*, Richard Mabey suggests that the youthful fishermen of the Isle of Man once used the milky juice of *Euphorbia helioscopia* for much the same purpose! Most gardeners, however, will find that the most irritating effect of the sap is to literally gum up the blades of secateurs when pruning plants. This only happens when using the scissor or by-pass type of secateurs. If you grow euphorbias a pair of anvil-cut secateurs will be much more suitable since the sap cannot stick the blades together. Always clean secateurs thoroughly after use because the dried sap can retain its toxicity for many years and even anvil-cut secateurs can seize up if the sap gets into the mechanism.

The origin of the name *Euphorbia*

The most widely quoted view is that of the authors of the *Oxford English Dictionary* and the unimpeachable Professor W. T. Stearn. They state that the word derives from Euphorbus, the name of a Numidian physician during the reign of Juba II, king of Mauretania, in the first century BC. Euphorbus may have used the sap of the native *Euphorbia resinifera* to burn warts from the hands of his patients. The name 'euphorbium' was used by Dioscorides in the first century AD to describe these plants and he suggested that the sap was good for 'griefs of ye hips' among many other things. John Raven, the Cambridge classicist, disputes this explanation, however, stating that the name is derived from the Greek for 'good fodder'. Although some euphorbias have been used as food after thorough drying, it is more common for euphorbias to be the only vegetation left after over-grazing by goats. It is difficult, therefore, to believe that they could be considered good fodder.

CULTIVATION

SOILS, SITING, PLANTING AND SUPPORTING

Euphorbias are an essential component of any garden and they are remarkably easy to cultivate. They are very tolerant of soil pH, do not require any obscure form of pruning or propagation and are relatively free of pests and diseases (see pp.29–33). There is a *Euphorbia* for every position in a garden – from dry to wet, sunny to shaded positions, through to sheltered or exposed sites – although not every *Euphorbia* grows everywhere or anywhere. Euphorbias may be used for their colour and texture or used to dominate as individual specimens, or they may form a backdrop for other plants. In the next chapter (see pp.34–45) there are suggestions for which species to grow in the various microclimates and situations of a garden.

As with all garden plants, good planting is essential to give the new plant a healthy start. In autumn or spring, dig a hole bigger than the root ball of the plant and fill the hole right up to the top with water. When the water has all drained away, place the plant in the hole with the top of the compost level with the soil. Half backfill the hole and compact the soil to the same firmness as the compost around the roots. Refill the hole with water and when this has drained away, finish backfilling the hole. Do not water the plant again unless it starts to wilt; repeated watering will lead to a shallow-rooted plant. This method of planting encourages the roots to grow further down into the soil.

Most herbaceous euphorbias will require some kind of support. If you have a supply of fresh bamboo shoots, make

Borders do not come much more mixed than this one in Jill Walker's Oxford garden. Euphorbia cyparissias and E. amygdaloides var. robbiae have reputations as invasive plants but they are good companions for Iris 'Green Spot', Prunus laurocerasus 'Otto Luyken' and Aucuba japonica f. longifolia 'Salicifolia'.

hoops from these around and across the *Euphorbia* clump. The hoops should then be tied together with raffia string. Birch or hazel stems woven into a cage over the crown is equally effective. Alternatively, stakes can be used which should support the plant to about two thirds of its final height. The advantage of using a natural material for staking is that the stake can be shredded along with the plant when it is cut back in autumn. Good staking should be as inconspicuous as possible, however, and so metal staking systems are also suitable if they are well hidden. Stake euphorbias in early spring so that it can be achieved without damaging the plant.

PRUNING

Euphorbias are divided into four groups (see below) and their successful pruning is dependent upon knowing into which group a particular plant falls. In the 'Species and Cultivated Euphorbias' section euphorbias are listed according to these groups. For pruning, it is advisable to use anvil-cut secateurs, to wear gloves and to take care not to allow sap to splash onto your skin or be rubbed into your eyes. *Euphorbia* prunings can be shredded and composted like any other garden waste.

Group 1: Annuals, biennial & short-lived perennials

No pruning whatsoever is required for these species. They will grow, flower, produce seed and die. At this point they should be pulled up and composted. If you do not want them to seed themselves around your garden then pull them up before the seed capsules start to explode.

Group 2: Herbaceous perennials

The above-ground parts of these plants die down to ground level each autumn, sometimes after spectacular autumn colour. The dead stems should be cut down to soil level when you think that they look unattractive. Less sap will flow from the wounds if you wait until early winter before doing this. In the following spring, new shoots will emerge from the crown of the plant or all over your garden in the case of *Euphorbia cyparissias*.

Group 3: Biennial-shooted evergreen perennials

This is the strangest group of euphorbias and there are few other groups of plant that have this growth form. They appear to be evergreen because there are always leafy shoots visible above the soil but the shoots are never more than two growing seasons old. These species flower at the end of shoots that were produced during the previous growing season. After flowering and fruiting, these two-year-old shoots die and are replaced by a new set of flowerless shoots that will flower during the next growing season. Pruning is simple; all you need to do is to cut

Fresh bamboo canes tied together with raffia make a very robust yet attractive frame through which herbaceous perennial species like Euphorbia villosa can easily grow.

23

out the dead flowering shoots as low as possible (normally to ground level) when you think that they look untidy.

Once flowering has finished (and seeds collected if required), the shoots that carried the flowers should be cut off as close to ground level as possible without removing the strong new shoots that will flower next year.

Group 4: Evergreen or deciduous shrubs

For these plants, pruning is only carried out for aesthetic or pragmatic reasons, such as when they grow too big. When the plant has finished flowering, the seed capsules will swell and eventually explode so if you want to prevent unwanted seedlings then cut off the flowerheads straight after flowering. These shrubs can often grow too big for their position but as it is common for them to produce new shoots from the centre, the plants may be cut back to these new shoots either straight after flowering or in spring after the risk of frost has passed.

PROPAGATION OF EUPHORBIAS

Propagation of euphorbias falls into three types: seed, shoot cuttings and division. Not all three methods are suitable for every species and propagation by seed is inappropriate for any named cultivated variety (or cultivar). Cultivars of euphorbias must be propagated by one of the two vegetative methods if the resulting offspring are to be true to their name. This is not to say that the seedlings resulting from named cultivars will not be good garden plants; they may, in fact, be better than the parent plant but they must not be distributed under the cultivar name if we are to maintain the genetic purity and accuracy of named forms. Research using genetic fingerprinting techniques has shown that many named cultivars are not genetically identical and it is often difficult to establish which plant is the original form.

Sowing seeds

Most euphorbias in cultivation, including the cultivars and hybrids, will set viable seeds. It has already been noted that euphorbias are pollinated by a wide variety of insects and other animals (see p.11) and as these pollinators are not species specific, the chances of pollen being deposited on a flower of another species are high, especially if you grow several different species in your garden. Natural hybrids are common in the wild where two euphorbias share the same habitat. Unless the parentage of a seedling hybrid is known, I recommend that you hoe it off or otherwise dispose of it because such hybrids simply add to the confusion that already exists in the naming and classification of euphorbias.

Hardy annual, biennial and half-hardy species, such as *Euphorbia stricta*, *E. lathyris* and *E. marginata* respectively, can only be propagated by seed. Seed of half-hardy euphorbias should be sown in mid- to late spring in a frost-free glasshouse or frame. This late sowing ensures that the seedlings emerge as the day length exceeds that of the night and the resulting seedlings are much stronger continuing to grow and flower into autumn.

Seeds of hardy species, whether annual, biennial or perennial, should be sown in proprietary seed compost between midwinter and early spring in a frost-free glasshouse or frame. Consistently good results can be achieved by sowing in soil-less seed compost. Viability rates of 90 per cent are not uncommon, and sowing two or three seeds in an 8cm (3in) pot is perfectly reasonable. If more than one seed germinates, simply leave the strongest seedling and pull out any others before they interfere with the seedling to be left. The advantage of this method is that the roots of the seedlings are not damaged because they do not need to be pricked out. As soon as roots appear through the drainage holes in the bottom of the pot, the young plant should be potted on into a 13cm (5in) pot. A soil- or loam-based potting compost, such as John Innes No. 2, is good at this point because the loam content improves the chance of the plant growing well when it is planted out in the garden which should take place when the roots start to emerge through the drainage holes of the second pot. Seedlings may suffer from attacks by pests and diseases and especially mildew; to control mildew, ensure that the air around the seedling is dry and that the plants are not being watered excessively. Young plants of the more tender species will benefit if kept in a frost-free glasshouse or frame through their first winter.

One final consideration to bear in mind when propagating euphorbias by seed is that the seed of most species has a notoriously short viability. *Euphorbia* seeds are often viable for just a few years. It is claimed that the British native *Euphorbia amygdaloides* has reappeared following woodland clearance where it has not been seen for 125 years, but this is exceptional. Do not expect good rates of germination from old seeds.

Stem cuttings

If you have a particularly good form of a species that you wish to increase, whether it be a named variety or just a form that does especially well in your garden, you can probably propagate it by stem cuttings. Take 6–8cm (2½–3in) cuttings in spring as new growth emerges near the base of the plant. This can be a

messy operation because the sap will be rising fast. Pushing the cutting into the soil around the plant can stop the bleeding from the base of the cutting, or you can use kitchen paper to mop up the sap. Keep the cuttings in a sealed polythene bag until you are ready to deal with them.

Cuttings of euphorbias respond very well to a hormone treatment, with the best results usually achieved with the fluid rather than powder preparations. Follow the instructions on the product and place six cuttings around the edge of a 9cm (3½in) pot filled with proprietary cutting compost to which you have added an equal volume of horticultural coarse sand. These cuttings should then be placed either in a closed frame or in a glasshouse. Alternatively, cover the pot with a bell jar or polythene bag. If bottom heat can be applied to the compost, in a heated propagator for example, then this will increase the strike rate. After six weeks, roots should have appeared through the drainage holes in the base of the pot. Pot up individual rooted cuttings into 8cm (3in) pots containing soil-based potting compost, such as John Innes No. 2, and later pot them on into 13cm (5in) pots in John Innes No. 3 potting compost if available. Plant out in the garden when the roots appear through the drainage holes once more. As with seed-raised plants, young plants of the more tender species will benefit if kept in a frost-free glasshouse or frame through their first winter.

Division

This method of propagation only works for the truly herbaceous perennials and for those evergreen species that send out runners. The propagation of the evergreen euphorbias that run, such as *Euphorbia amygdaloides* var. *robbiae*, is very easy. Simply dig up and pot rooted runners into soil-based potting compost such as John Innes No. 3. This can be a good source of plants for fund-raising plant sales and Christmas presents.

Euphorbia Division

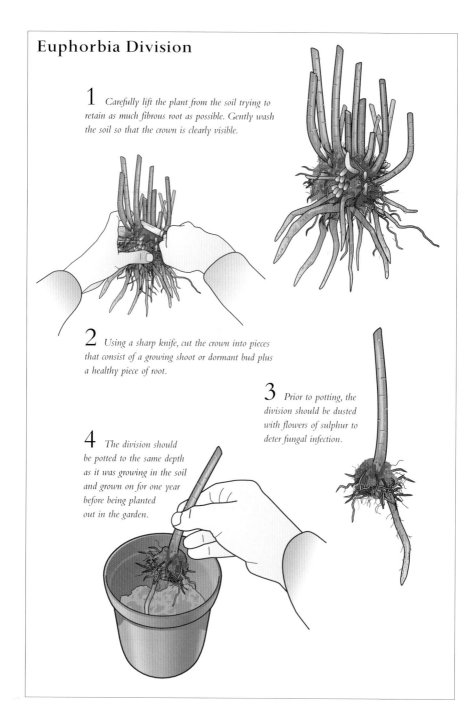

1 *Carefully lift the plant from the soil trying to retain as much fibrous root as possible. Gently wash the soil so that the crown is clearly visible.*

2 *Using a sharp knife, cut the crown into pieces that consist of a growing shoot or dormant bud plus a healthy piece of root.*

3 *Prior to potting, the division should be dusted with flowers of sulphur to deter fungal infection.*

4 *The division should be potted to the same depth as it was growing in the soil and grown on for one year before being planted out in the garden.*

There are also herbaceous species that appear to run, such as *E. sikkimensis* and *E. griffithii*, but these 'runners' may not have any roots on them.

Unfortunately, division of herbaceous perennial euphorbias is not as straightforward as it is for other herbaceous perennials such as hostas or asters. Put away thoughts of placing two border forks back-to-back and gently easing the dormant clump into two pieces and do not even think of slicing the plant down the middle with a sharp, clean spade. Herbaceous euphorbias have a thick woody rootstock that broadens near its top, giving rise to the mass of shoots in the spring. If this is torn apart, it will rot quickly. The way to divide these plants is to lift the whole crown out of the ground and carefully remove the soil. Then, cut the crown into sections with a sharp knife, each with a piece of shoot and root, and dust the cut surfaces with flowers of sulphur to reduce the chance of fungal infection. Finally, pot up the divisions into 13cm (5in) pots in soil-based potting compost, such as John Innes No. 3, and grow them on for one year before planting out. Division is not a technique that should be used to propagate the biennial-shooted evergreen perennials such as *Euphorbia characias*, *E. myrsinites* and *E. nicaeensis*.

PESTS AND DISEASES

Euphorbias are generally free of pests and diseases, although rusts and powdery mildew may occasionally be serious. Pesticides are rarely needed in a garden setting. The following six problems are the most common:

Aphids

Aphids feed by inserting their hypodermic-needle-like mouthparts into the vascular tissue (internal plumbing) of a plant. The aphids ingest a sugary solution and often engorge themselves to such a degree that 'honeydew' seeps out of the rear of the aphid falling onto the leaves below. Black, sooty mould (a non-parasitic fungus) grows on the sticky honeydew disfiguring and weakening the plant. It is a constant surprise to gardeners that aphids are able to avoid the tissues that contain the sticky white sap and insert their mouthparts into the

vascular tissue. Individual *Euphorbia* species are often infested by their 'own' specific types of aphid. If you can resist the temptation to reach for the pesticide container there may be a natural increase in predators of the aphids and the aphids will never become a serious problem. As with many pests and diseases, plants are most suspectible when they are young seedlings and during the flowering period. Since the aphids are green they are often unseen. Rubbing them off seedlings by hand is perfectly practical on a small scale. If necessary, spray plants with an appropriate pesticide.

Red spider mites

These mites only become a problem in glasshouses or outdoors in warm, dry summers. The symptoms of a severe infestation are curled, dying leaves covered with a fine web. Tiny, yellowish green or orange-red mites will be just visible with the naked eye. This problem can be suppressed with a regular (twice-daily if possible) spray with water from a hand-sprayer or hose pipe. When this is not possible, if the plant is in front of a window for example, then patience is required. This country is rarely dry and warm long enough for the plant to be killed by this pest. As the humidity rises and the temperature falls, the plant will recover. This is most commonly a problem on *Euphorbia mellifera*. Pesticides against red spider mite are rarely effective because of the evolution of pesticide resistance. If there is a serious problem with this pest, an effective treatment is to introduce a predatory mite, *Phytoseiulus persimilis*, before a heavy infestation has developed. The predator is available by mail order from suppliers of biological controls.

This plant of Euphorbia mellifera *is suffering from an infestation of red spider mites. Three weeks later, after two days of steady rain but without the application of pesticides, the problem had cleared and the plant was growing very healthily.*

Thrips

These little insects suck sap from leaf surfaces, leading to unsightly russet-coloured patches on the leaves. These wounds may then become infected with pathogens like fungi. A severe infestation on seedlings can be fatal. *Euphorbia stygiana* seems to be the most susceptible species. The use of predatory mites, *Amblyseius* spp., can be highly effective especially if the plants are in a propagating frame or glasshouse and the predators are introduced before a heavy infestation has developed.

31

An appropriate pesticide can be tried as an alternative to biological control.

Mildews

There are two forms of this disease – powdery and downy. The former is worse in dry years and the latter in wet seasons. Euphorbias are particularly vulnerable to both of these fungal diseases when they are seedlings. If you have pricked out enough seedlings, you can allow the susceptible seedlings to die thereby helping to select resistant individuals. Some varieties are particularly vulnerable to mildews even when fully grown. One of these is *Euphorbia amygdaloides* 'Purpurea' and many gardeners who wish to avoid the use of pesticides choose not to bother growing this plant. There are plenty of other better purple-leaved herbaceous perennials. Several fungicides are available to gardeners for control of powdery mildews but their use is seldom necessary. There are no fungicides available to gardeners for downy mildew.

Rusts

Rusts often have several very different stages in their life cycles but it is the orange-brown pustules on leaves and stems that are the most commonly seen. If you grow *Euphorbia dulcis* 'Chameleon', it is very likely that your population of plants will eventually succumb to rusts and there are no resistant forms yet available. Several fungicides are available to gardeners to control rust.

When a plant becomes so common and widely planted so quickly after its discovery, it is easy to forget what was grown for purple foliage before the new plant was available. There are many good purple-leaved plants to replace *E. dulcis* 'Chameleon' if it consistently fails to succeed in the garden. *Heuchera micantha* var. *diversifolia* 'Palace Purple' is one such plant, as is *Anthriscus sylvestris* 'Ravenswing'. If one wants to avoid the use of pesticides then you have to accept that sometimes an alternative plant has to be found. No one should be so devoted to growing euphorbias that they have to get the pesticide bottle out every two weeks.

Euphorbia dulcis 'Chameleon' is very prone to infection with rust fungus and many gardeners have given up growing this form.

32

PLACING EUPHORBIAS IN GARDEN SITUATIONS

HERBACEOUS BORDERS

The choice of which herbaceous *Euphorbia* to use in your garden depends on the size of your border. The most common herbaceous species, however, is *Euphorbia polychroma* and its varieties. Its cyathium leaves are such a clean yellow that they combine very well with other plants in either harmonious yellows and oranges or with contrasting blues and purples. For a harmonious effect, grow *E. polychroma* with *Tulipa linifolia* Batalinii Group 'Bright Gem', *Helianthemum* 'Henfield Brilliant', Solomon's seal (*Polygonatum odoratum*) and bronze fennel (*Foeniculum vulgare* 'Purpureum'). The picture can be further improved with *Papaver orientale* 'Saffron' and *Euphorbia griffithii* 'Fireglow', which start to flower a few weeks later, and *Nectaroscordum siculum* flowers even later again as the bronze fennel grows taller.

Contrasting displays that set the yellow cyathia leaves of *Euphorbia polychroma* against purples and blues include the use of the leaves of purple sage (*Salvia officinalis* 'Purpurascens') and the blue flowers of *Centaurea montana* and *Camassia leichtlinii*. *Euphorbia villosa* can be used to great effect as a large plant at the back of the border and any of the species with dark leaves, such as *Euphorbia donii*, *E. cognata* and *E. wallichii*, provide a perfect backdrop to other colours. For example, *E. wallichii* is the perfect companion to the pink harmonies of *Thalictrum aquilegiifolium*, *Centranthus ruber* and *Persicaria bistorta* 'Superba'. On a smaller scale for a smaller garden, the combination of *Euphorbia cognata* with *Dictamnus albus* var. *purpureus* gives a strong yellow and rich pink

The garden at Hadspen House in Somerset is one of the best places to see many euphorbias used brilliantly in a variety of borders. Sandra and Nori Pope have used both Euphorbia griffithii 'Dixter' and 'Fireglow' with E. polychroma at the top of Sandra's graduated colour border.

contrast for weeks in the summer. At the end of the season, both *Euphorbia villosa* and *E. palustris* are useful in herbaceous borders as they extend interest well into autumn with their vivid flame colours.

MIXED BORDERS

Euphorbia characias seedlings, *E. polychroma*, *E. villosa* and *E. palustris* can all be grown together as ingredients of a yellow mixed border. Such borders are dominated by a huge variety of different yellows, and the euphorbias can be used to add their tones along with a choice of other yellow flowers and leaves of which there are far too many to mention by name. The tiniest specks of blue, however, provided by the likes of blue forms of *Aquilegia vulgaris* will lift a yellow mixed border and create even more excitement.

A fascinating combination of *Euphorbia* × *martinii*, *E. amygdaloides* 'Purpurea', *Ajuga reptans* 'Braunherz', blue geraniums and rosemary has been used brilliantly in gardens with the blues bringing the purples and reds in the euphorbias into focus. A similar combination of colours can be created much later in the year when the leaves of the purple forms of *Euphorbia characias* combine with the leaves of *Geranium renardii* and the flowers of *Aster amellus* 'Veilchenkönigin'. A more gentle combination for full sunshine is *Euphorbia polychroma* and *E. amygdaloides* var. *robbiae* with *Prunus laurocerasus* 'Otto Luyken', *Aucuba japonica* f. *longifolia* 'Salicifolia' and *Iris* 'Green Spot'.

Mixed borders are often the best places to use the shrubby euphorbias like *E. mellifera* and *E. stygiana*. The honey scent of the former makes this an obvious choice for beneath a window or by an entrance. The dark foliage of the latter is a great background and complement to other strong foliage plants such as *Acanthus sennii* or *Eryngium giganteum*. The front of mixed borders can become a problem because the plants must not be too tall or they will obscure the other plants but they need to be tough enough to compete with shrubs. *E. amygdaloides* var. *robbiae* is one such plant for a shaded position while *E. myrsinites* or *E. rigida* are perfect for the front of a sunny border.

This picture shows a small section of the yellow borders at Hadspen House. Euphorbia polychroma and E. palustris are just two of the yellow plants shown to perfection with the addition of small amounts of blue.

BOG AND WATER GARDENS

Several euphorbias, especially the Himalayan species, produce a much better garden plant if they are grown in a bog or water garden surrounding a pond. The most extreme example of this is *Euphorbia griffithii* in its various forms. This plant must have a soil that does not dry out if it is to remain compact. Where it is grown around a pond with its roots in soil, it produces dense mounds that look more like a shrub than a herbaceous perennial. *E. griffithii* 'Dixter' looks magnificent with *Iris sibirica* 'Butter and Sugar' and *Carex elata* 'Aurea' (syn. 'Bowles' Golden'). This latter sedge also works very well with *Euphorbia palustris* and *Iris pseudacorus*.

When Euphorbia griffithii *is grown in very moist soil, such as by this water-lily covered pond in the Van Dusen Botanic Garden, it forms very dense clumps rather than running through the soil.*

ROCK GARDENS

Several good euphorbias come from the Mediterranean region and many of these are very happy in a rock garden. The choice, however, depends on the size of the rock garden. *Euphorbia characias* is often found in the wild growing on rocky slopes, but it will only look in proportion in a large rock garden with large rocks. An advantage of a rock garden is that small plants, such as *E. capitulata*, can be seen easily and nurtured; the same plants in a mixed border could easily be swamped.

Many of the blue-leaved species appreciate the extra heat that rocks emit. *Euphorbia brittingeri*, *E. myrsinites*, *E. portlandica*, *E. pithyusa*, *E. rigida* and *E. seguieriana* all flourish in a well-drained spot between rocks. *E. paralias* is a very good plant for dry sunny places especially if the soil is impoverished. *E. spinosa* is a good specimen plant whereas *E. pithyusa* looks wonderful with a blue-flowered creeper like *Campanula portenschlagiana* growing beneath it.

Probably the best *Euphorbia* for a sunny position on a rock garden is *Euphorbia myrsinites* because of the way that it works with other colours. A particularly harmonious combination is *E. myrsinites* underplanted with a dark-flowered form of *Iris reticulata* although the iris must be planted deep (more than 10cm (4in)) if it is to flower each year. The leaves of the iris are

Euphorbia myrsinites forms the perfect background for Iris reticulata 'Wentworth' in full sunshine in a rock or gravel garden.

long and very thin and do not interfere with the *Euphorbia*. Next to the *E. myrsinites* you may plant *Allium senescens* var. *glaucum* which has grey-green leaves and pale mauve flowers and this combination can be improved by *Convolvulus sabatius* with pale blue flowers. *Euphorbia myrsinites* also looks very good next to *Tulipa turkestanica*. A less subtle and very exciting contrast can be seen between the yellow cyathium leaves of *E. myrsinites* and the yellow flowers of *Cytisus* × *praecox*, and the pink and yellow flowers of *Tulipa saxatilis* Bakeri Group 'Lilac Wonder'. Both of these combinations can be reproduced in large containers.

GRAVEL GARDENS

More than just a thin layer of stones on the soil, a gravel garden can be a very effective horticultural device for setting off Mediterranean plants that like to grow in full sunshine with very sharp drainage around their crowns. The colour of the gravel should be considered carefully for maximum effect. After double digging the soil and levelling it to give a smooth surface, evenly spread a layer of sand over the soil, followed by a layer of gravel over the sand, each layer 8cm (3in) deep. The gravel and sand layers will help to smother any germinating weed seeds while providing a good seed bed for the seeds of many of the species that like to grow in a gravel garden.

The following euphorbias are very suitable for growing in a gravel garden:

E. barrelieri	E. mellifera
E. capitulata	E. myrsinites
E. characias in all its forms	E. polychroma and its
E. lathyris	cultivars
E. × martinii	E. rigida

Euphorbia
polychroma *can be
grown successfully
with many other
plants but few are as
successful as this one
with* Tulipa batalinii
'Bronze Delight'.

HOT AND DRY GARDENS

In addition to the species that are suited to gravel gardens, some euphorbias grow best in a rich soil in full sun. These species can be grown very effectively with tulips of a befitting colour. The choice of colour is very personal, but most people find *Euphorbia polychroma* with the various forms of *Tulipa linifolia* Batalinii Group very attractive. This is a good association because this tulip does not need to be replaced annually, which is the case with more highly bred varieties. *Euphorbia rigida* and *E. nicaeensis* are both best grown in the sunniest of places in the garden. The former is a voracious feeder and some people mulch this with well-rotted farmyard manure to great effect. *E. ceratocarpa* makes a better garden plant if grown in full sun because the stems turn a very bright red colour. The advantage of growing *E. mellifera* in full sunshine is that the nectar glands around the flowers are warmed up, and its honey scent is very much enhanced.

41

The following euphorbias are very suitable for growing in hot and dry gardens:

E. acanthothamnos	*E. nicaeensis*
E. characias in all its forms	*E. paralias*
E. corallioides	*E. polychroma* and its
E. × *martinii*	cultivars
E. mellifera	*E. rigida*
E. myrsinites	*E. seguieriana*

EXPOSED AND COASTAL GARDENS

A large number of our garden euphorbias grow naturally around the coast of southern Britain and southern Europe. These places may be windy, but they are frequently less prone to frosts. *Euphorbia paralias* is only seen growing in sand dunes where it is well adapted to the shifting sands and *E. portlandica* is a common site on cliffs and stable dunes. *E. characias* is often found at the back of these dunes. *E. spinosa* and *E. acanthothamnos* can be grown in full sunshine in seaside gardens in parts of southern Britain and Ireland, but not elsewhere without winter protection.

The following euphorbias are very suitable for growing in exposed and coastal gardens:

E. characias in all its forms	*E. paralias*
E. × *martinii*	*E. portlandica*
E. mellifera	*E. spinosa*

SHADY SITES AND WOODLAND GARDENS

Euphorbia paralias
*is a very common
sight on the sand
dunes in southern
Portugal where
very few other
plants can survive.*

The classic *Euphorbia* for a shady or woodland situation is *Euphorbia amygdaloides* var. *robbiae* and it looks good backed with *Mahonia aquifolium* or *Viburnum davidii*. It can be grown to great effect in a 'wilderness' border and allowed to compete with butterbur (*Petasites*) and Solomon's seal (*Polygonatum*). Seedlings of *Euphorbia corallioides* could also be scattered through the area where they may self-sow.

In the wonderful woodland beds at Cambridge University Botanic Garden, there is a fantastic combination of *Euphorbia polychroma*, *Persicaria bistorta* 'Superba', *Euphorbia* × *martinii*, blue hardy geraniums and white heucheras. A slightly brighter association sees *Euphorbia palustris* growing through a carpet of English bluebells (*Hyacinthoides non-scripta*). In this informal setting, *E. palustris* does not require staking. The combination of *Euphorbia griffithii* 'Fireglow' with English bluebells is an acquired taste but it may work for you!

CONTAINER DISPLAYS

Many euphorbias will grow very happily in a variety of containers from large pots to hanging baskets. *Euphorbia myrsinites* is one of the best for hanging baskets and *E. polychroma* can also be used but these should never be hung in such a position that they might brush against peoples faces. In pots, *E. myrsinites* can be combined with a variety of other plants such as bulbs; those tulips suggested for rock gardens (see p.40) are also recommended here.

The more tender species like *Euphorbia acanthothamnos*, *E. glauca*, *E. dendroides* and *E. mellifera* are all suitable subjects for container cultivation. In regions where they will not survive outside, they can be moved under cover and given winter protection. All of these species grow well in soil-based potting compost, such as John Innes No. 3, but if they are to be in the same pot for more than one year, add extra grit to the compost to prevent waterlogging.

The cyathium leaves of Euphorbia barrelieri *put on a very good show of pink in late summer, especially when the plant is grown in a container.*

SPECIES AND CULTIVATED EUPHORBIAS

There are more than 200 different euphorbias available in the British nursery trade. The more common or garden-worthy species and varieties are described below and they are listed here in the same four groups as used in the 'Cultivation' section on pages 23–24. Within these groups, the species and varieties are listed in alphabetical order. Unless stated otherwise, assume that these plants are hardy down to -29°C (-22°F) and the stem leaves will not be mentioned unless they are either useful identification features or they contribute to the garden appeal of the plant. Euphorbias are rarely grown for their leaves alone although the silver leaves of *Euphorbia myrsinites* and others or the dark green leaves of *E. amygdaloides* var. *robbiae* are desirable features when the plants are not in flower.

GROUP 1: ANNUALS, BIENNIALS AND SHORT-LIVED PERENNIALS

Euphorbia biumbellata

This upright species from the eastern half of the Mediterranean region is best treated as an annual plant and should be propagated by seed sown each year in the spring. It grows to approximately 50cm (20in) tall with a spread of 40cm (16in) and is happiest in full sun in rich, well-drained soil. The name is a misnomer because it does not have two umbels; an umbel is a type of flowerhead not found in euphorbias. This species has two whorls or rings of cyathia on short stems, one above the other. The cyathium leaves are khaki-yellow

The yellow cyathium glands of Euphorbia cognata *are a perfect contrast for the purple of thalictrums and alliums.*

46

making a good companion to many other colours throughout the summer.

Euphorbia corallioides

This upright biennial or short-lived perennial has an open
growth habit and a well-founded reputation for being fussy
about where it will live. It is easily propagated by seed; if it
grows in your garden, it will seed itself and you will never have
to sow it again. If you have not planted it in the right place,
however, it will peter out and not produce any flowers or seeds.
One situation that it accepts is a very free-draining, rich soil
in full sun. Happy plants will grow to 1.4m (4½ft) tall with a
spread of up to 70cm (28in). The open, much branched
flowerheads account for at least half of the height of the plant.
Towards the end of the plant's life there may be no stem leaves
left on the plant. Almost all parts of the plant, including the
immature seed capsules, are hairy when new and fresh but as
the plant matures the hairs are shed from the older parts.
The stems and leaves, especially the leaf undersides, are suffused

The distinctive coloration of the cyathia, glands and flowers of Euphorbia glauca *make it one of the best for seeing the structure of euphorbia inflorescence.*

with pink giving the whole plant a coral-coloured hue. It flowers from spring through to the first frosts in autumn. When weeding, be careful not to remove the next generation of seedlings from around the base of old plants. It has the same geographical distribution as *E. ceratocarpa* and they will grow very happily alongside one another.

Euphorbia glauca

This short-lived perennial comes from the south end of the South Island of New Zealand where it is reduced to just three populations. A mature plant in Britain will grow to 60cm (24in) tall with a spread of 50cm (20in) but it is most successfully grown in a 30cm (12in) container being brought into a frost-free greenhouse for the winter. The most remarkable features of *Euphorbia glauca* are the cyathia and their flowers in summer. These are devoid of cyathium leaves and are bright red with bright burgundy horned nectar glands around the rim of each cyathium. The male stamens are also bright red with vivid yellow pollen and the female flowers are dull green – a contrast that allows the flowers and cyathia to be seen easily. The stem leaves are a clean silver-blue. As a garden plant, this species is best grown as a specimen in a pot but the compost should never be allowed to dry out. New plants are best grown from seed.

Euphorbia lathyris

When identification keys are written for the spurges cultivated in British gardens, this biennial is nearly always the first to be keyed out; it is the only hardy species with the stem leaves in opposite pairs with each pair at a right angle to the pair below. The leaves on a young plant can be a deep marbled green. This is one of the species that will be either very happy (seeding itself around) or weak and feeble preferring a rich, well-drained soil that never completely dries out. In the first year, it grows to about 1m (3ft), then rests during winter, growing into an upright plant 2m (6ft) or more tall in the second year with a huge, greenish yellow flowerhead up to 1m (3ft) in diameter. This flowers right through summer and into early autumn. On a sunny day in late summer, the seed capsules – the largest of any frost-hardy *Euphorbia* – explode with a very clearly audible 'crack'. This species can only be propagated by seed and this is best done by allowing the plant to sow itself. Seedlings in the wrong place can then be moved or potted up for sale or presents when 5cm (2in) tall. In the UK, it is known as caper spurge or mole-wort. The former name refers to the fleshy part of the immature seed capsule, which can be used as a very poor substitute for capers although the seeds are toxic. The origin of mole-wort is discussed on page 18. *E. lathyris* was originally confined to central and eastern Asia but it has now become naturalized in many other countries including Britain.

Euphorbia marginata

Very few spurges from North America have made it into British gardens but this is one of the best. It should be treated as a half-hardy annual with seeds sown in mid- to late spring in a frost-free greenhouse. The advantage of sowing seeds at this time is that the plants continue to look healthy and flower through summer right into the autumn. If sown too early, the plants begin to look straggly by late summer. The seedlings will be stronger and will transplant more successfully if the seeds are sown in John Innes No. 1 potting compost. Plant out the

The variegation on the leaves of the half-hardy annual Euphorbia marginata *provide light patches in borders through to the end of summer.*

resulting seedlings only when the risk of frost has passed completely. Sow two seeds in an 8cm (3in) pot and pinch out the weaker seedling if both seeds germinate. The leaf variegation is a good clean white and if all variegated plants were this good they would not receive such a bad press. This species is named for the foliage; there is a white border to all of its leaves — stem, ray and cyathium and the plant is sometimes known as snow-on-the-mountain. The nectar glands around the rim of the cyathia are small and pale yellow but they have a relatively large white, petal-like growth up to 5mm (¼in) in diameter. This results in the cyathium and flowers resembling a true flower more closely than any other *Euphorbia*. The plant needs full sun and a nutrient-rich soil that never dries out, performing best if farmyard manure is dug into the soil the previous winter. It should make bushy growth 1.2m (4ft) tall and 40cm (16in) wide. In frost-free regions of the world this species can be grown as a short-lived perennial growing to 1.5m (5ft) tall.

Euphorbia stricta

This annual or very short-lived, compact and bushy perennial has the capacity to become a bit of a weed by seeding itself around with great enthusiasm. It grows in any soil in partial or dappled shade or full sun, reaching up to 80cm (32in) tall, although it is more commonly 50cm (20in) tall. The plants may have one or many stems that are often crimson and contrast well with the pale green or almost yellow stem leaves. The flowerheads are much branched and the mass of cyathium leaves give a bright pale yellow cloud of colour from late spring to early autumn. Seeds of *Euphorbia stricta* are sometimes sold under the name 'Golden Foam' and seed is the only suitable means of propagation.

GROUP 2: HERBACEOUS PERENNIALS

Euphorbia altissima

One task that many gardeners could live without is staking. This robust and non-spreading herbaceous perennial, which grows to 1.5m (5ft) tall with a spread of 75cm (30in), does not require any support when grown in rich, well-drained soil in full sun or dappled shade. The cyathium leaves are yellow and provide colour in late spring and summer. In its native range of the eastern Mediterranean to Iraq, it dies back in summer but in Britain it holds its leaves into autumn. This fine plant gives herbaceous borders volume and weight especially in a yellow and blue border. Propagate by seed and stem cuttings in spring or by careful division in autumn.

Euphorbia brittingeri (syn. *E. verrucosa*)

This species has a large geographical range from Spain across to Hungary and it varies in height and spread. It is normally a low-growing plant rarely reaching more than 15cm (6in) tall but it spreads 50cm (20in) from its crown. The stem leaves are small (3cm (1¼in) long by 1cm (½in) wide) and dark green. In contrast, the cyathium leaves are deep golden yellow and are at their best in summer. It can be grown in full sun or shade requiring a fertile, well-drained soil. Propagate by seed and stem cuttings in spring or by careful division in autumn.

Euphorbia cognata (syn. *E. cashmeriana*)

This is a delicate, upright herbaceous species that deserves to be grown more widely. Originating from the western end of the Himalayas and surrounding countries, it grows to 70cm (28in)

Dictamnus albus *var.* purpureus *flowers simultaneously with* Euphorbia cognata *and the yellow and purple form a classic contrasting colour combination.*

in neat clumps 50cm (20in) wide and rarely requires staking when grown in a herbaceous border in moisture-retentive but well-drained, rich soil. The smallish leaves (5cm (2in) long by 1.5cm (⅝in) wide) are dark green with well-defined cream central veins. The cyathium leaves are very bright yellow throughout summer even when the plant is grown in partial shade. It looks particularly effective when associated with dark-purple-flowered plants. Propagate by stem cuttings in spring or by careful division in autumn.

Euphorbia cornigera (see also *E. wallichii*)

Sometimes two similar species become so confused in cultivation that the truth of their identity can become completely obscured. The situation is further compounded if the species have an overlapping geographical range and if they are used in exactly the same situations in our gardens.

53

This is the case with *Euphorbia cornigera* and *E. wallichii*. The former is from northern Pakistan and Kashmir while the latter has a wider distribution from Afghanistan to China. *E. cornigera* is smaller, rarely growing more than 60cm (24in) tall and 50cm (20in) wide but this can be more in very favourable situations on rich, moisture-retentive soil. It requires support even in a full herbaceous border. The dark green leaves are a good foil to other plants and the green-yellow cyathium leaves provide some colour from late spring to the end of summer. Propagate by stem cuttings in spring or by careful division in autumn.

Euphorbia cyparissias

Some plants acquire a bad reputation through no fault of their own and this is very much the case with this species. In the past, gardening books have suggested that because this is one of the smaller euphorbias, growing to about 30cm (12in) tall, it is suitable for a rock garden. If your rock garden covers 2 acres (1 hectare), like the one in the University of Utrecht Botanic Garden, then it will be fine. Most of us do not have this space, however, so planting this species in a rock garden is lunacy. *Euphorbia cyparissias* spreads by rampant underground runners and it grows through winter; in spring, it can emerge up to 75cm (30in) away from where it was last seen the previous autumn. The natural range of this species is Europe down to Turkey but it has escaped from gardens in North America and become naturalized there. It has not yet become an invasive species but given the current paranoia in the USA with alien invasive weed species, it may soon appear on their federal list of undesirables. It shares many characteristics with other plants that are now major problems elsewhere in the world. This does not make it a bad garden plant, of course, and in the right place it provides colour for a longer period than any other species of *Euphorbia*.

Euphorbia cyparissias is happiest in full sunshine in any soil but it will tolerate some shade from other herbaceous plants growing around it. It is smaller that most species with narrow leaves 4mm (⅛in) wide that end in a sharp point. These are crowded onto the lax stems in an easily discernable spiral arrangement. The delta-shaped cyathium leaves are bright yellow when the plant is in full flower in spring. As the male

The subtlety of Euphorbia dulcis complements the bright yellow cyathium leaves of E. cyparissias to the benefit of both species.

flowers are shed and the seed capsules develop and explode, the cyathium leaves turn to bright red. The stem leaves also change to bright yellow and often have red tips. This colour can extend into mid-autumn, meaning that this plant gives good strong colours for six months of every year. It must not be condemned just because someone once advised planting it in a rock garden. Some people prefer to cut the plant right down in early summer for two reasons: firstly, this stimulates vigorous fresh growth which stops herbaceous borders looking tired in late summer and early autumn; secondly, it takes some of the vigour out of the plant and slows its progress underground.

There are a number of good cultivated varieties. 'Orange Man' grows up to 45cm (18in) tall and has especially good stem leaf autumn colour of the cleanest yellow. 'Bushman Boy', on the other hand, is a compact form that has smaller stem leaves than the true species. There is now just one variety with purple leaves, namely 'Fens Ruby'. In the past, the names 'Clarice Howard' and 'Purpurea' have been used but the plants were indistinguishable from one another. As is the case with other purple-leaved varieties, the colour is best if the plants are grown in full sun and expect the colour to fade to dark green in summer. In spring, however, the purple leaves form a striking backdrop to the bright yellow cyathium leaves although it should be said that yellow and purple is not everyone's cup of tea. Following flowering, a new crop of vegetative shoots appears at the top of the plant giving it a fresh appearance into late summer and autumn. Propagate by stem cuttings in spring but can also be easily divided at almost any time of year.

Euphorbia donii (syn. *E. longifolia*)

All gardeners appreciate the need for a well-defined set of rules for naming plants and it is obviously unacceptable for one species to have two names. When this happens, the name that was given first must be used (assuming that the first name was used legitimately and according to the rules). Despite this, it is always irritating when an unfamiliar name is resurrected or created to replace a familiar name. It is even more galling when the name being replaced is descriptive of the plant and the new name commemorates an unknown person. This is true of

Euphorbia donii which was formerly known as *E. longifolia*. In 1825, George Don used the name *E. longifolia* illegitimately for this species. The name was illegitimate because it had already been used for a Canary Island species (*E. mellifera*) in 1788; Don did not do his homework properly. In 1989, Robertus Oudejans discovered this illegitimacy and renamed this species after the man who got it all wrong in the first place; a Christian act if ever there was one and far more than Don deserves.

Euphorbia doniii is a striking, upright herbaceous plant from Nepal, Bhutan and Tibet and it will easily grow to 2m (6ft) each year. It needs to be staked and will seed freely so be careful when weeding in spring as the seedlings emerge. If there is no room in the border for these to develop, they can be potted up when they are approximately 8cm (3in) tall. The leaves are much longer than they are wide, sometimes more than 15cm (6in) long and just 3cm (1¼in) wide. They are dark green with a central cream stripe. The flowerhead is yellow with cyathium leaves just 5mm (¼in) wide providing colour throughout

The cyathium leaves of Euphorbia donii *bring a classic euphorbia Chartreuse colour to the herbaceous border in mid- to late summer.*

summer. This plant is very tolerant of a range of situations and will grow equally well in a dry gravel garden or in moist soil. A recent introduction from Pakistan has been given the cultivar name of 'Amjilassa' after the name of the village near the collection site. Its seeds are available with proceeds being returned to the villagers as *per* the spirit of the 1992 Convention on Biological Diversity. Propagate by seed and stem cuttings in spring or by careful division in autumn.

Euphorbia dulcis

This is a much underrated species that has been overshadowed by its purple form 'Chameleon' for the last decade. It makes a very neat hemispherical dome, 30cm (12in) in diameter and is particularly well suited to growing in dry conditions by the side of stone steps or in cracks in paving. It prefers full sun but will tolerate some dappled shade. Loosely branching flowerheads emerge from the dome of shoots in late spring with the cyathium leaves the same matt green as the stem leaves. In autumn, the cyathium leaves turn red, yellow and orange making a significant contribution to the autumn colour in the herbaceous border.

The millions of plants of 'Chameleon' that were to be seen in nearly every garden at the end of the twentieth century all arose from one purple-leaved plant collected from a ditch in France. The eagle-eyed lady concerned received not one penny for her introduction. Had she benefited, she might now be giving it all back because the plants began to die out after a decade due to infection by a rust fungus. Since there is no spray to control the rust, 'Chameleon' is possibly on its last legs unless a resistant mutant develops. This story illustrates the problems associated with raising a huge population of plants from such a small gene pool of just a single plant. The absence of any significant genetic diversity means that there is no real chance of a resistant individual being present in the population. Propagate by seed and stem cuttings in spring.

Euphorbia esula (see also E. × pseudovirgata)

If there was ever a plant that should never be brought into a garden, it is this one. A drift of ground elder has more appeal

because at least ground elder is edible. This species resembles a giant *Euphorbia cyparissias* without the colour and charm. It is, in fact, a close relative and has been known to hybridize with it; the result being known as *E. × pseudoesula*. It runs underground, it is impossible to stake or support in any way, and it is dull green all over. Do not under any circumstances think of growing or propagating this weed; bare soil has more appeal.

Euphorbia griffithii

This is perhaps the most superficially distinctive of all the hardy euphorbias in cultivation by virtue of the orange colour of its flowerheads from mid-spring to early summer. The cyathium leaves are bright orange, the round nectar glands are pale yellow, and even the stems are orange, especially when young. It will not grow well on dry soils, however, because the drier the soil, the more it runs, leading to a very sparse appearance but if growing by the side of a pond it forms a dense stand like a hedge. It grows up to 1m (3ft) tall in good moist soil in full sun; in shade, the plants are shorter. Propagate by stem cuttings in spring or by careful division in autumn.

The best known cultivars are 'Dixter' and 'Fireglow'. The latter has pale green stem leaves and orange cyathium leaves. 'Dixter' has stem leaves with a grey-purple hue and an orange-pink central vein and the cyathium leaves are deep flame orange. 'Fireglow' is slightly taller than 'Dixter' when both are grown side-by-side but since the final height is so dependent upon moisture and nutrient levels in the soil, it is meaningless to compare their heights in different situations and gardens. In its native habitat in the mountains at the eastern end of the Himalayas, the range of colours seen in *Euphorbia griffithii* is much greater than those found in cultivation.

Euphorbia nereidum *will grow to 2.75m (9ft) tall as here in Bristol University Botanic Garden in association with* Lavatera *'Barnsley'.*

Euphorbia hyberna

The Irish spurge is native to western and south-western Europe including the British Isles. Its horticultural appeal lies in its compact habit and dark leaves. Both the cyathium and stem leaves are dark green and the flowers appear from late spring through summer. It is happy in shade, dry or moist, where it will grow to 90cm (36in) tall with a spread of 45cm (18in) and it will seed itself around the garden. It is not a stunning garden plant but it is one of those perennials that gives weight and volume to a herbaceous border. Propagate by seed and stem cuttings in spring or by careful division in autumn.

Euphorbia jacquemontii *has a unique purple edge to its leaves which is made more obvious when this species is grown with purple flowered plants.*

Euphorbia jacquemontii

This Asian native from Pakistan to Tibet was first named in 1862 but it has only recently re-appeared in cultivation in Britain. It is a delicate species forming narrow clumps that grow to a height of 50cm (20in) with a spread of just 30cm (12in). It grows in dappled shade but is better in full sun on rich soil that never dries out completely. It is the stem leaves that are the most remarkable feature of this species; the edge or margin of each leaf is luminescent purple, appearing to

glow like the flowers of corn cockle (*Agrostemma githago*). The rest of the leaf is a marbled grey-green. This is one *Euphorbia* that is mainly grown for its foliage and is best associated with purple-flowered plants, thereby making the edges of the leaves more obvious. The yellow cyathium leaves are produced in the second half of summer. Propagate by stem cuttings in spring.

Euphorbia nereidum

Most of the euphorbias that grow in Morocco are succulent species, but this is a herbaceous plant of awesome proportions especially when compared to *Euphorbia jacquemontii*. In dappled, dry shade, it grows to 2m (6ft) but in a sheltered corner in moist soil it exceeds 3m (10ft) with a stem so robust that staking is unnecessary. As a native of Morocco, you might be suspicious of the hardiness of this species, but it has survived -10°C (14°F) in central England without any protection. The use of dried bracken or some other form of winter insulation will guarantee its survival in frost-prone areas. In a mild winter, the flowering stems will continue to bear flowering cyathia throughout. It can be distinguished from all the other herbaceous euphorbias by its impressive height and it spreads by runners rather than as an ever-increasing clump. The cyathium leaves are a clean yellow which contrasts well with plants with clear pink colours. Propagate by seed and stem cuttings in spring or by careful removal of runners in autumn.

Euphorbia oblongata

Best described as a clumping herbaceous perennial that does not really have a dormant spell, this is a short plant rarely exceeding 60cm (24in) with a spread of 50cm (20in). It produces an endless succession of new shoots that terminate in a flowering head of the clearest yellow throughout the year.

The warty seed capsules are produced in such profusion that the plant will spread over your entire garden very quickly if allowed. One thing that sets this species apart from most other herbaceous euphorbias is its ability to thrive and multiply in shady, woodland conditions. Cut off all the top growth to rejuvenate old plants. This is best done in spring but it can work at any time of year. Propagate by seed sown in spring.

Euphorbia palustris (see also E. villosa)

The specific epithet of this species implies that it suits damp, bog-like situations. In its huge geographical range from Europe to north-western China, it certainly does grow in damp conditions in some countries but always remember that damp is a relative term. What is regarded as damp in one country may be relatively dry in another. For gardeners, this means that this is a very versatile Euphorbia; it will grow in a dry border at the base of a wall as well as on the edge of a pond (but better not if that pond contains fish). If grown in damp conditions and full sun, it may not need support because the tall shoots, up to 2m (6ft), are so strong and thick but when grown in drier situations, it will collapse untidily in midsummer so staking is essential. A properly supported plant attains a spread of 1.5m (5ft). This species shares with Euphorbia villosa the ability to produce the most superb autumn display of orange and red from its stem leaves after flowering in late spring and early summer. It further resembles E. villosa by producing a flush of non-flowering growth in mid- to late summer from the top of the flowering shoots, also after flowering. The leaves are relatively large, reaching 20cm (8in) in length, and the flowerheads are deep yellow. Propagate by stem cuttings in spring or by careful division in autumn.

Euphorbia polychroma (syn. E. epithymoides)

This Euphorbia provides a true, bright yellow when it flowers in spring, all over the perfect dome. It grows to 60cm (24in) with a spread of 50cm (20in) unless you plant one of the more vigorous varieties like 'Major' and 'Sonnengold' which grow to 80cm (32in) tall and 60cm (24in)wide. The latter of these two

Blue and yellow is a very popular contrasting combination; here Camassia leichtlinii is grown with Euphorbia polychroma and Centaurea major.

has especially large, very bright yellow flowerheads and is a good form of an already very good garden plant. This species requires either full sun or dappled shade but does not like heavy shade or permanently moist soil in which it may rot. As the seed capsules mature, they turn yellow with sausage-like protrusions tipped with pink. The specific name *polychroma* refers to the many autumn colours of the stem and cyathium leaves. 'Candy' has young foliage suffused with purple in spring although this colour is short-lived as the sun bleaches them back to the usual green. The variegated form 'Lacy' has a white border to its leaves, but you must plant this in full sun if you want it to survive. It is a good plant for a container because you can hide it when it starts to look scruffy. Propagate by stem cuttings in spring or by careful division in autumn.

Euphorbia x *pseudovirgata*

There are many well-documented examples of how the hybridizing activities of gardeners have led botanical taxonomists (classifiers) and nomenclaturists (namers) to re-examine their work. Many gardeners have struggled for a number of years to distinguish between *Euphorbia esula* and its various subspecies, *E. virgata*, *E. waldsteinii* and the hybrid *E.* × *pseudovirgata*. The latest expert view is that these species and hybrids are just variations on the theme of *E. esula*. Earlier, *E. esula* is described as a plant of no horticultural merit whatsoever and the same can be said of the other plants listed above. But this may not be fair. There are plants in the nursery trade, offered under the name of either *E. waldsteinii* or *E.* × *waldsteinii* that are valuable when grown in containers. In these growing conditions, it reaches just 60cm (24in) tall with a spread of 30cm (12in) with narrow stem leaves and relatively small yellow cyathium leaves in summer. The container prevents the plant from spreading in a wanton way. If you grow plants in containers and want a yellow herbaceous perennial this is a worthy choice. Propagate by stem cuttings or by division in autumn.

Euphorbia sarawschanica

As so many euphorbias are in cultivation, there is often a species that is just right for a particular place in your garden. If you are

looking for a robust, yellow herbaceous perennial that flowers throughout summer and grows to 2m (6ft) tall in full sun or slight shade, this may be the one for you. *E. sarawschanica* is a reliable plant from central Asia that will never be a star in its own right but it is a worthy member of the chorus and should be included in any border that requires an ensemble performance. The clump quickly reaches 70cm (28in) in diameter in average soil and in all but the most crowded and sheltered borders, it requires some form of support. Propagate by seed and stem cuttings in spring or by careful division in autumn.

The recent discovery of Euphorbia schillingii *in the 1980s proves that there are still good garden plants waiting to be discovered and domesticated.*

Euphorbia schillingii

The practice of naming newly discovered species after the gardener who first introduced the plant into cultivation is a fine

tradition. It ensures that many unsung heroes of British gardening achieve a degree of immortality. This is the case with *Euphorbia schillingii*, named after Tony Schilling, who was for many years the inspiration behind the development of the botanical garden at Wakehurst Place in Sussex. The plant was collected in central Nepal and is a clump-forming herbaceous perennial that achieves a height of 85cm (34in) with a spread of 50cm (20in). It prefers full sun and a good soil that never dries out completely and it is happy in a container. The stem leaves have a pale green stripe down their centres, in common with many of the Himalayan species and the flowers and cyathium leaves are produced later than many species with the height of the colour in the second half of summer. The cyathium leaves are yellow and together the pairs form an almost perfect circle. Propagate by seed and stem cuttings in spring or by careful division in autumn.

Euphorbia sikkimensis

This is one of the easiest euphorbias to identify; when the shoots re-emerge in early spring they are bright cerise-pink and this distinctive colouration also extends to the stem leaves. Once the shoots have grown to about 30cm (12in), the stem leaves lose their flush of youth and develop a more regulation green but the stems and central veins of the stem leaves retain their pink hue. This species runs through the soil and the drier the soil, the more it runs. If you want a compact plant, therefore, grow it in moist soil that never dries out. The plant easily reaches 2m (6ft) in a season and spreads quite widely. The cyathium leaves are at their most colourful in the first half of summer making it the earliest of the Himalayan species to make a contribution to the garden. Propagate by stem cuttings in spring or by careful division in autumn.

Euphorbia soongarica

This is another tough *Euphorbia* from southern European Russia across to Mongolia. In many ways it is a shorter, stocky version of *Euphorbia sarawschanica*, growing to 1.5m (5ft) tall in a season with a spread of 1m (3ft). It only needs staking in the most exposed of situations and is happy in full sun or partial

shade and it tolerates a range of soil conditions. Like its compatriot *E. sarawschanica*, this species plays a supporting role in the herbaceous border flowering in the middle of summer. Propagate by seed and stem cuttings in spring or by careful division in autumn.

Euphorbia villosa (see also *E. palustris*)

Many gardeners struggle to tell the difference between the close relatives *Euphorbia villosa* and *E. palustris*. When they are in their first flush of flower in late spring it is simple because the young seed capsules of *E. villosa* are covered in silky hairs whereas those of *E. palustris* have no hairs. The differences stop there. These flowers are produced in late spring and for most of the summer when the greenish yellow cyathium leaves are at their most colourful. This is a good species for a large herbaceous border on all but the driest soils and is valued for its flowers in spring and summer and for its yellow autumn foliage. *E. villosa* grows to 2m (6ft) and forms large clumps with a spread of 2m (6ft) but it will always need some form of support. There is a hybrid between *E. palustris* and *E. villosa* that goes by the name of *Euphorbia × jablonskiana* but it is sadly not in cultivation. As garden plants, the parent species are interchangeable and may be forms of the same species. Propagate by stem cuttings in spring or by careful division in autumn.

Euphorbia virgata see *Euphorbia × pseudovirgata*

Euphorbia wallichii (see also *E. cornigera*)

This large herbaceous perennial easily grows to 1.2m (4ft) in a season with a spread of up to 1m (3ft). The dark green stem leaves have pale central veins and the first cyathium leaves are often borne in threes giving rise to a triangular appearance and are khaki-gold in colour. The height of flowering is in midsummer. The plant tolerates some shade but if the shade is too dense then the plant will decline and die, especially if the soil is prone to drying out. Propagate by seed and stem cuttings in spring or by careful division in autumn.

The contrast of the stem and cyathium leaves of Euphorbia amygdaloides *'Purpurea' makes this a splendid specimen plant when it does not become infected with mildew to which it is very prone.*

Euphorbia ✕ *waldsteinii* see *Euphorbia* ✕ *pseudovirgata*

GROUP 3: BIENNIAL-SHOOTED EVERGREEN PERENNIALS

Euphorbia amygdaloides

Wood spurge is one of the most common euphorbias in our gardens. It is a British native species and is frequently found in shady areas at the edge of deciduous woodlands or in clearings. You are more likely to come across the atypical variety *Euphorbia amygdaloides* var. *robbiae*, however, than the true type *E. amygdaloides* subsp. *amygdaloides*. The latter is an evergreen species which grows to a maximum of 60cm (24in) tall with a spread of 45cm (18in) and greenish yellow cyathium leaves which are at their most colourful in spring and early summer. The stem leaves are softly hairy and form a dense spiral of leaves on each shoot in their first growing season. These shoots produce a flowerhead in the following spring. When the flowers are over and their seeds have been expelled from the capsules, the whole shoot should be cut off to ground level. Unlike most euphorbias, the wood spurge seeds can remain viable for long periods while they wait for a clearing to form when a tree in their native woodland collapses. Seeds have been observed to remain viable but dormant in the soil for 125 years.

Euphorbia amygdaloides subsp. *amygdaloides* is a 'clumper', i.e. it does not send out runners of any form and retains a neat, non-invasive shape. The same cannot be said of the common *E. amygdaloides* var. *robbiae*. This variety was discovered in a wood outside Istanbul by a Mrs Robb, who recognized this form as a good garden plant and brought a piece back to England in her hat box; this gave rise to the plant's common name of Mrs Robb's bonnet. It differs in many ways from the English native species. The foliage is very dark green and shiny rather than pale green and hairy and the cyathium leaves tend to be a clearer yellow although they are produced at the same time in spring and early summer. It is the propensity of var. *robbiae* to run vigorously, however, that really sets it apart; this is not a plant for a small garden, but it is one of the best groundcover plants for dry shade. Mrs Robb's bonnet does well

underneath trees like planes (*Platanus*) which are notorious for drying out and starving the soil around their roots and it can even survive around the edges of conifers. The plant is robust and tolerates being kicked and trodden on so it suits the side of a public footpath or pavement and it will be equally happy in sun or shade although it runs even more in full light. Propagation is easy by simply potting up the runners making it a good plant to grow if you need to supply charity plant sales. If it does become invasive, it is easy to remove and does not grow again from small root fragments left in the soil.

Euphorbia amygdaloides subsp. *amygdaloides* closely resembles a small *E. characias*, and it should come as no surprise that these two form natural hybrids, known collectively as *E.* × *martinii*. Since this is a naturally occurring hybrid, there are as many forms of *E.* × *martinii* as there have been hybridizations. As yet, there are no records of *E. amygdaloides* var. *robbiae* hybridizing with *E. characias*. The progeny of such a union might be a bit scary resembling *E. amygdaloides* var. *robbiae* on steroids!

A number of red- to purple-leaved forms of *E. amygdaloides* exist with 'Purpurea' being the most common but in some gardens this plant is a complete waste of time as it is very susceptible to mildew, especially in wet years. In total contrast to its parent species, 'Purpurea' performs very well in full sun in well-drained soils; it also does well in containers filled with free-draining compost and in dry shade. A well-grown plant of 'Purpurea' is a wonderful sight with the bright yellow, fused cyathium leaves contrasting beautifully with the purple foliage. Occasionally a variegated form appears in nurseries but these are always sickly plants that quickly die and rarely make a long-term contribution to any garden.

Euphorbia barrelieri

The cyathium leaves of Euphorbia barrelieri *bring an eye-watering red to the garden in late summer.*

This spurge is found growing in the northern Mediterranean region from France to north-western Turkey. It has a slightly untidy growth habit, as if it cannot make up its mind whether it is an upright or prostrate plant. It has blue-green foliage arranged in a loose spiral and the cyathium leaves, produced through summer, are a similar colour. Towards the end of summer, the foliage becomes tinged with red and the cyathium

71

leaves turn a magnificent cerise-pink. *Euphorbia barrelieri* deserves to be grown more widely. It performs best in a scree bed or rock garden, in a gravel garden or in a container, preferably in full sun but it will tolerate some shade for part of the day. It will not tolerate moist soil. Propagate by seed and stem cuttings in spring.

Euphorbia capitulata

A rock garden in full sun or dry dappled shade and dry soil is required for this odd species from the Balkan peninsula. The leaves are less than 1cm (½in) long and only 5mm (¼in) wide. The stems are prostrate and just 20cm (8in) long and in their second year they end with a circular head of cyathia about 1cm (½in) in diameter. This is such an unusual feature that another name for this species is *Euphorbia soliflora* but *E. capitulata* is the correct name. This is a species for the collector rather than an ornamental garden. Propagate by seed and stem cuttings in spring.

In the cold of the winter the leaves of Euphorbia characias *subsp.* wulfenii *'Purple and Gold' give a rich solidity to a mixed border.*

Euphorbia characias

This is possibly the most common *Euphorbia* in British gardens and not without justification. There are more named cultivated varieties of this species than of any other *Euphorbia* with more than 35 different forms listed in the *RHS Plant Finder*. They are all bushy plants and vary from 1–2m (3–6ft) tall and wide. The flowering times vary so much that it is possible to have varieties in flower at any time of the year, including winter with types like 'Perry's Winter Blusher'. In part, this plant owes its diversity to the

Euphorbia characias 'Burrow Silver' is one of several variegated forms of this species but it is the least hardy.

fact that it is a very variable species in its natural range from Portugal to Turkey. At the eastern end of the Mediterranean, wild plants *tend* to have bluish, hairy leaves with yellow-horned nectar glands around the rim of the cyathia. These plants were originally described and named as *Euphorbia wulfenii*. At the western end of the Mediterranean region, wild plants *tend* to have green leaves with dark red or purple nectar glands on the rim of the cyathia. These were described and named as *E. characias*. As gardeners travelled more widely and introduced plants of these two 'species' into cultivation, it became apparent that they hybridize freely, giving rise to many different forms, all of which produce fertile seed. It is clear, therefore, that the two names apply to forms of the same species. *E. characias* is the legitimate name because it was used before *E. wulfenii*. Strictly speaking, the two forms described above are known as *E. characias* subsp. *characias* and *E. characias* subsp. *wulfenii*. There really is no significant difference, however, between populations of *E. characias* at the two extremes of their natural range so the division of the species into two subspecies is not really relevant or helpful.

Cultivars have been selected from plants of both of the subspecies. Some of these were selected for the colour and texture of their stem leaves, 'Blue Hills' for example; some for the colour of their cyathium leaves, such as 'Lambrook Gold'; and some for the colour of their nectar glands, like 'Black Pearl'. All of these cultivars produce copious quantities of viable seed and there is an irresistible temptation to distribute seedlings under the name of the parent cultivar. As a result of this sloppy nomenclature, it is impossible to be entirely confident about the accuracy and authenticity of the names of most of the cultivars currently offered in the nursery trade. This is not important in a garden setting since it is the appearance of the plant that is important and not the name and many of the seedlings from the cultivars are very good garden plants.

Cultivars selected for their foliage colour or texture tend to be authentic since they must be propagated by cuttings taken in spring to retain their colour. *Euphorbia characias* 'Portuguese Velvet' is a compact, semi-prostrate plant with the most wonderful silver-haired leaves. *E. c.* subsp. *characias* 'Blue Hills' is a fine, neat plant 1.2m (4ft) tall with blue stem leaves borne in profusion. *E. c.* subsp. *wulfenii* 'Purple and Gold' has purple leaves which are particularly striking in the cooler temperatures of late autumn, winter and early spring but as the temperatures rise, the purple flush fades; the gold of the name refers to the golden cyathium leaves. Inevitably there are variegated varieties with 'Emmer Green' and 'Burrow Silver' being the best, although the former is hardier. All foliage forms of *E. characias* are ideally suited to sunny, sheltered situations.

Cultivars selected for the colour of their cyathium leaves or nectar glands are more variable. 'Lambrook Gold' has golden cyathium leaves and 'John Tomlinson' has bigger flowerheads but the cyathium leaves are more yellow. Two more forms worthy of mention due to their size are 'Humpty Dumpty', a compact plant rarely exceeding 75cm (30in) tall with tight flowerheads having dark purple, almost black nectar glands, and *E. characias* subsp. *wulfenii* var. *sibthorpii* (or 'Sibthorpii' for short) at the other end of the size scale. 'Sibthorpii' grows to 2m (6ft) or more with blue-grey stem leaves and bright yellow nectar glands and its spread can be more than 2.5m (8ft) if there is space for the outer shoots to fall outwards, thereby creating a large, hemispherical dome. While Humpty Dumpty is well known, John Sibthorp is less famous. He was Professor of Botany at the University of Oxford at the end of the eighteenth century and the author of the most beautiful book ever produced: *Flora Graeca* with illustrations by Ferdinand Bauer. The plates of the euphorbias of Greece and the Aegean are especially beautiful and perfectly accurate in every detail.

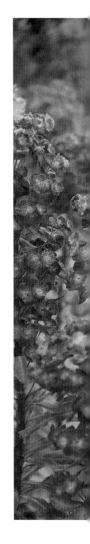

Euphorbia ×
martinii 'Red
Dwarf' is an
undervalued garden
plant with red
cyathium leaves that
look bright for
many months.

In summary, *Euphorbia characias* is a very variable plant. The stem leaves may be any colour from purple through green to blue and the nectar glands vary from yellow with long horns through to a shiny-black rhomboid shape. The cyathium leaves, however, are nearly always fused together into a cup, in the centre of which sit the cyathia. Most forms of the plant prefer a sunny situation with free-draining soil but many perform well in dappled shade. Remove the shoots after flowering to the woody base of the plant to create room for the new shoots that will flower in the following year. Old plants can become very congested at the base and it is sensible to try to cut away all the dead twigs near the woody base of plants to promote the growth of strong, young shoots. In its many forms, this species has an unfounded reputation for being tender; plants growing in Oxford in the winter of 1981–82 tolerated temperatures as low as -29°C (-22°F). In addition to an undeserved reputation for tenderness, it is believed by some that this is a short-lived plant and yet there are many plants that have survived for more than 20 years.

Euphorbia × *martinii*

This naturally occurring hybrid between *Euphorbia characias* and *E. amygdaloides* subsp. *amygdaloides* has been recorded many times, in and out of cultivation. Since both parents are variable in their habits, especially *E. characias*, the hybrids are also very variable although *E.* × *martinii* is an almost a perfect intermediate form of its parents. It can be regarded as either a large *E. amygdaloides* subsp. *amygdaloides* or a small *E. characias*. The crescent-shaped nectar glands are often red with the pigmentation spreading into the cyathium leaves and stems and the flowerheads are normally more open than either parent. A plant in full flower, at any time from mid-spring to early autumn, is unlikely to reach more than 1m (3ft) in height or spread. One parent grows best in full sun and the other in shade but fortunately this hybrid grows almost anywhere with the possible exception of wet soil. 'Red Dwarf' is the one really good cultivated variety. Its cyathium leaves fade to a rich matt red and retain their colour for many months. Propagate by seed and stem cuttings in spring.

When hybrids form between two species, there is often the chance that the offspring will hybridize with one of the parents. The plants that result from this 'back cross' will be a new combination of the characteristics of the parents, with a bias towards the parent involved in the back cross. 'Redwing' is one such complicated hybrid and the parents are thought to be *Euphorbia* × *martinii* and *E. characias* subsp. *wulfenii* 'Purple and Gold'. 'Redwing' is a first-rate garden plant and is especially effective in large containers where its plum-red coloration can be matched with foliage and flowers of other plants.

Euphorbia myrsinites

This native of dry mountain regions of southern Europe and across into northern Iran is one of the finest euphorbias for a sunny position in a rock garden, a well-drained border or a container (including hanging baskets and wall-mounted mangers). Its pale blue stem leaves are approximately twice as long as they are wide and are arranged in clearly discernable spirals on the stems. They often drop off as the flowerhead matures. The leaf size is one of the key differences between this species and *Euphorbia rigida* whose leaves are normally four times longer than they are wide. The green-yellow cyathium leaves are at their best in the second half of spring. Soon after the seed capsules start to explode and distribute their seeds, the new shoots growing from the base become clearly visible. The old shoots that have finished flowering must be removed although the timing of this pruning really depends on whether you want the plant to set seed. If you are happy for *E. myrsinites*

When grown in full sunshine, in well drained soil, there are few better silver-blue leaved plants than Euphorbia nicaeensis.

to multiply and spread then it is much easier to do this by self-sown seedlings than to raise plants in containers from collected seeds or by stem cuttings. Vigorous specimens may have a spread of 1m (3ft) but 60cm (24in) is more common. Plants normally reach 20cm (8in) tall. This species has a reputation for being short-lived but 10-year-old plants are not uncommon.

Euphorbia nicaeensis

Although the specific name correctly implies that this species is a native of southern France around the town of Nice, it is a variable species with nine subspecies and varieties that encompass north-western Africa, Turkey and the Caucasus area, as well as south-western Europe. When grown well in full sun in nutrient-poor soil, there are few better bushy plants with silver-blue foliage. The bright red stems contrast well with the stem leaves and the cyathium leaves are at their best in late spring. These are normally silver-green but subsp. *glareosa*, from the eastern end of the species' natural range, has colourful, strong khaki cyathium leaves which are at their best in midsummer. This subspecies reaches just 30cm (12in) tall whereas the true species grows to 60cm (24in) tall with a similar spread of 50cm (20in). Since *E. nicaeensis* is primarily grown for its foliage, prune away the flowering shoots as soon as they start to look a bit scruffy. Propagate by stem cuttings taken in spring.

Euphorbia paralias

This is one of the most distinctive and remarkable plants to be seen on the seaward edge of the shifting sand dunes of the Algarve region of southern Portugal. You may come across this plant, however, on the dunes of southern Britain and Ireland and many other countries in western and Mediterranean Europe as well as the Canary Islands. This is not a particularly hardy species, surviving down to just -10°C (14°F). Nor is it a surprise to learn that this species needs a well-drained soil but this makes it a very useful plant because it tolerates extremely dry soil, including that found under pine trees where precious few plants grow well. The small, grey-blue stem leaves are very distinctive and up to 2.5cm (1in) long and 5mm (¼in) wide and they are held at an angle of 45 degrees or less, densely clothing the stem. This is an adaptation to reduce water loss from the plants in their hostile habitat. The pale silver-blue cyathium leaves appear in early summer. The plant grows to 60cm (24in) tall and 50cm (20in) wide. The roots do not normally run through garden soil and the plant forms clumps as a result. When it grows on sand dunes, however, the roots do run and the thick, woody rootstocks are often exposed when the sand shifts; if you see these, you will understand why the division of *Euphorbia* clumps using a pair of border forks back-to-back does not work. Propagate by seed and stem cuttings in spring or by careful division in autumn.

Euphorbia portlandica

Portland spurge is found in a very similar range to *Euphorbia paralias* but in a very different habitat. *E. portlandica* grows in rock fissures and on dry scree slopes around the coasts of western

The Mediterranean species Euphorbia rigida likes the sunniest position available.

Europe in full sun. The blue-grey, spatula-shaped stem leaves, slightly curved like a spoon, are borne in distinct spirals and, like the stems, they are often flushed dark red. The delta-shaped cyathium leaves are pale silver-blue and are at their most profuse in late spring; the nectar glands are yellow with thin horns. It makes a small, prostrate plant: up to 15cm (6in) tall with a spread of 30cm (12in) at the most. Propagate by seed in spring.

Euphorbia rigida

This Mediterranean species is found growing in north-western Africa, southern Europe, and across Turkey and into Iran, always in sunny positions. It is a large version of *Euphorbia myrsinites* with several important differences: it is too big for most rock gardens because it spreads more than 1m (3ft) across with a maximum height of 50cm (20in). The stem leaves are up to 8cm (3in) long and 1.5cm (⅝in) wide with a distinct point and the cyathium leaves are a strong, deep yellow, similar in shade to the yellow portion of the foliage of *Euonymus fortunei* 'Emerald 'n' Gold'. The cyathium leaves are at their most colourful in spring, and the yellow-green nectar glands have wart-like growths on their edges. There are some forms, as yet unnamed, with

79

cyathium leaves that turn deep red in late summer. In common with many other Mediterranean species, the stem leaves of *E. rigida* are borne in distinct spirals. Give this species the sunniest spot in the garden with no shade and as it is a hungry plant, mulch the soil around their base with well-rotted farmyard manure. In the right situation, it will seed around like *E. myrsinites*, often into the cracks between paving stones. Propagate by seed or stem cuttings in spring; cuttings with a piece of old wood at their base may root more effectively.

Euphorbia seguieriana *is a delicate little spurge that is best grown in full sun in a rock garden or in a container.*

Euphorbia seguieriana

This *Euphorbia* has a wide geographical distribution and a large number of described subspecies and forms. It is found from Europe across to Pakistan in sunny, exposed places and in

gardens it needs full sun and well-drained soil. The stem leaves are blue-green and narrow (up to 6cm (2½in) long and rarely more than 1cm (½in) wide) and the cyathium leaves are at their most attractive in the first half of summer with lime-green cyathia. It forms a dome with a radius of 40cm (16in). This is a species that produces a great quantity of viable seeds and will sow itself around a rock garden. Propagate by seed and stem cuttings in spring. In contrast to the other blue-leaved species that flower on biennial shoots, this is a more delicate and lax plant, often with a clearly visible woody base from which the shoots arise. The form most commonly offered by nurseries is subsp. *niciciana*, which is barely distinguishable from the true species. If you have one then you do not need the other unless you are trying to collect as many different euphorbias as you can.

GROUP 4: EVERGREEN OR DECIDUOUS SHRUBS

Euphorbia acanthothamnos

This is an eastern Mediterranean shrub for growing either in a sheltered, well-drained position in relatively warm areas such as the south of England or in a glasshouse, preferably frost-free, elsewhere. The plant eventually grows at a rate of 5cm (2in) a year to a maximum size of 50cm (20in) tall and 1m (3ft) across. It has small, insignificant flowerheads in late spring. The main aesthetic reason for growing this species is its chicken-wire-like branching pattern, upon which are borne small leaves up to 1cm (½in) long. These leaves are often shed in summer and this can scare the first-time grower who fears that the plant is dying but the plant comes back into leaf quickly. In its normal habitat of rocky places, this is an adaptation to enable the plant to survive the hot, dry summers typical of Mediterranean regions. If grown in a container, use a soil-based potting compost, such as John Innes No. 3, with 25 per cent added grit to give a rich, free-draining growing medium. The small seed capsules (up to 2.5mm (½in) across) are covered in warts but it is rare for the seeds to be viable. Propagation is best carried out using stem cuttings in spring.

Euphorbia ceratocarpa

Some species of *Euphorbia* have a wide distribution and others narrow. This species is only found in Sicily and southern Italy and not surprisingly it needs a sheltered, sunny, well-drained site. If this is provided, then the plant will repay you well. It is a delicate shrub, 60cm (24in) tall and wide, with wiry red stems and dark green stem leaves. The cyathium leaves are bright yellow and are best in the second half of summer. *Euphorbia ceratocarpa* is good for borders around a house since it fits under most windows without obscuring the light and it grows very happily with *E. corallioides*. Propagate by seed and stem cuttings in spring.

Euphorbia dendroides

The tree spurge is a native of the Mediterranean region and the Canary Islands. It is a plant for a frost-free conservatory in all but mild areas, such as London and south-western England, and if you grow it in a container, it should be stood outdoors during summer because it appreciates full sun and fresh air. It grows up to 3m (10ft) tall with a spread of 1.5m (5ft). Like *Euphorbia acanthothamnos*, it is a summer-deciduous species with new leaves in mid-autumn. The yellow-green cyathium leaves appear in spring and turn bright red then fall in late summer.

Euphorbia dendroides *is a common sight in Crete and in the summer the cyathium leaves turn red before being shed to reduce water loss. This is a fine specimen plant for a container in a frost-free conservatory.*

Euphorbia mellifera is grown either for its foliage or for the strong honey scent given off at flowering time, by the nectar glands. It needs a sheltered position or a mild garden to perform well.

Oddly the nectar glands around the rim of the cyathia resemble a stylized cat's head. Propagate by seed and stem cuttings in spring.

Euphorbia mellifera

It is a truth universally acknowledged that a gardener in possession of a sheltered, sunny position must be in want of *Euphorbia mellifera*. Honey spurge is unrivalled for its scent and in late spring on a sunny day the air around a plant in full flower is suffused with such a strong aroma that it is as if someone has dropped a jar of honey nearby. The scent is derived from the nectar glands and the nectar is very attractive to ants which are often seen on the flowerheads jealously guarding their 'larder' from any other potential pollinators. The glands are without horns and vary in colour from yellow to fox-brown. The cyathium leaves are very small and drop off as the flowerheads mature and the pale green stem leaves reach 30cm (12in) long if grown in moist, mild areas in dappled shade. In dry soil and full sun, the leaves will be half this length or less. The mature seed capsules are up to 5mm (¼in) in diameter and are covered in warty protrusions. They can be heard exploding on sunny days and the resulting seedlings are voracious feeders; watering with a liquid feed and potting on into nutritious compost avoids malnutrition and makes for stronger plants. Propagate by seed and stem cuttings in spring.

Honey spurge is hardy to about -10°C (14°F) but hardiness depends on the individual plant. Some are undeniably more hardy than others. The need for a sheltered position often leads to plants being grown near to buildings or walls, places that are often dry for periods in summer. This can have two results: firstly, it makes plants susceptible to infection by red spider mites and secondly, the top of a mature plant over 2m (6ft) tall can dry out and die. The symptoms of both problems are the same. While the former problem is normally cured by the rain and falling temperatures of autumn, the latter is not. A mature plant whose top has died due to drought can be rejuvenated if cut back to the strong shoots that often appear near the base of a plant suffering from drought-induced die-back.

Plants of *E. mellifera* can grow to 5m (16ft) where the soil rarely dries out and where the air has a high humidity such as south-western England and parts of Ireland. In these situations, the leaves may grow almost as long as they do in their native homelands of the Canary Islands and Madeira. This feature lead to this species being named *E. longifolia* the year before it was given the name *E. mellifera*. If you have already read the account of *E. longifolia* on page 56 then you will know that the name of the herbaceous perennial that we formerly knew as *E. longifolia* is now *E. donii*. If the International Code of Botanical Nomenclature is applied ruthlessly, the plants that we all know as *E. mellifera* should be called *E. longifolia*. This would lead to great confusion but there is a provision in the code for technically incorrect names to be conserved if the consequences of the confusion are likely to be greater than the benefit of technical correctness.

The blue of the
flowers of
Campanula
portenschlagiana is
a perfect backdrop for
the blue-silver leaves
of Euphorbia
pithyusa.

Euphorbia pithyusa

Anyone who has read gardening books written more than 50 years ago will know that they often recommend plants that are no longer available in the nursery trade. This regrettable state of affairs was one of the reasons for the founding of the National Council for the Conservation of Plants and Gardens in the late 1970s. One function of the duties of National Plant Collection holders is to ensure that the rarer species are well established in many gardens and preferably in the nursery trade. Nurseries are vital in the process and it was Beth Chatto's nursery in Essex that re-introduced this unique species into cultivation. It was first described in 1753 and is a small Mediterranean shrub that grows to 1m (3ft) wide or more with a height of 50cm (20in).

85

It is happiest in full sun with very well-drained soil. The stem leaves grow to 2.5cm (1in) and are blue-grey and pointed. The lower branches become bare, however, so this *Euphorbia* is best grown in association with creeping herbaceous plants, such as *Campanula portenschlagiana* or rock-garden bindweeds (*Convolvulus* spp.). The cyathium leaves are also blue-grey but the nectar glands are burnt orange. Propagate by seed and stem cuttings in spring.

Euphorbia spinosa

This shrubby Mediterranean species needs a sunny, well-drained situation. In a cold winter, when the temperature falls below -10°C (14°F), it becomes deciduous and looks thoroughly miserable. The best plant in Britain is to be seen growing on the awesome limestone rock garden in the Cambridge University Botanic Garden, where the plant has a spread of more than 1m (3ft) and a height of 30cm (12in). The stems of *Euphorbia spinosa* are red with dark green stem leaves. The stem leaves are rarely more than 3cm (1½in) long with pale central veins and the cyathium leaves are either very small or absent when the plant is in full flower in early summer. Propagate by seed and stem cuttings in spring.

Euphorbia stygiana

This evergreen shrub from the Azores, first thought to be a form of *Euphorbia mellifera* but described as a new species in 1844, is currently in demand by discerning gardeners. It grows to 70cm (28in) tall and 1m (3ft) wide after five years and the leaves are dark green with pale central veins, superficially resembling those of a rhododendron. During a cold winter, the older leaves turn brilliant crimson. The cyathium leaves are deep yellow but they fall off before the seed capsules start to swell. The flowers are borne in early summer and smell faintly of honey. This plant grows best in a sheltered position that does not dry out, although sites that are sheltered and moist are unusual, so if *E. stygiana* is growing where the soil does dry, it may wilt during a dry summer. A suffering plant is quickly revived by a bucket of water. Although this species prefers a sheltered position, it is hardy down to at least -20°C (-6°F).

One of the best specimens of Euphorbia spinosa *grows on the rock garden at Cambridge University Botanic Garden, where it benefits from the shelter and protection of the limestone grikes.*

Propagate by seed and stem cuttings in spring. It occasionally hybridizes with *E. mellifera* if the two species are grown in the same vicinity; the flowering periods just overlap, with pollen from the last male flowers on *E. mellifera* pollinating the first female flowers on *E. stygiana*. The resulting hybrids produce fertile seeds so they need more than a cultivar name; they are currently given the working name of *E.* 'Devil's Honey'. The hybrids are more vigorous than either parent but they appear to be less hardy than *E. stygiana*. The hybrids take exception to frosts below $-5°C$ (23°F) but do not totally die at the base and they grow back in spring.

The foliage of Euphorbia stygiana *is reminiscent of some rhododendrons and it is a first class shrub for a mixed border.*

FURTHER INFORMATION

There are more than 200 different euphorbias available in the British nursery trade. Many garden centres stock euphorbias, usually when they are in flower, and several specialist nurseries offer a diversity of species and varieties. The *RHS Plant Finder* is the best place to start hunting for the less common forms.

AWARDS

The following euphorbias have received the RHS Award of Garden Merit (AGM):

> *E. amygdaloides* var. *robbiae*
> *E. characias* 'Portuguese Velvet'
> *E. cornigera*
> *E. Excalibur* ('Froeup')
> *E. griffithii* 'Dixter'
> *E.* × *martinii*
> *E. milii* (not hardy)
> *E. myrsinites*
> *E. palustris*
> *E. polychroma*
> *E. polychroma* 'Major'
> *E. schillingii*
> *E. sikkimensis*
> *E. Redwing* ('Charam')

Euphorbia griffithii *'Fireglow' is one of the most distinctive of all the hardy euphorbias due to the stunning orange colour of its flowerheads.*

BOOKS

There are a number of books that mention euphorbias. The writings of Beth Chatto, Penelope Hobhouse, Andrew Lawson, Christopher Lloyd, Piet Oudolf, Sandra and Nori Pope and Graham Stuart Thomas contain a wealth experience of where to grow euphorbias and with what to associate them with regards to colour. There is no real substitute for seeing the plants growing in gardens, however, and gardens where euphorbias grow in a variety of conditions include: the Royal Botanic Gardens Kew, the Royal Botanic Garden Edinburgh, RHS Garden Wisley, Cambridge University Botanic Garden, University of Oxford Botanic Garden, Hadspen Garden and Nursery in Somerset, East Lambrook Manor in Somerset, and Bury Court in Hampshire.

There are two books devoted to euphorbias. *Euphorbias: A Gardeners' Guide* by Roger Turner (ISBN 0-7134-8384-9), and the *Hardy Plant Society Guide to Euphorbias* by Don Witton (ISBN 0-9016-8716-2) who holds one of the National Plant Collections of hardy euphorbias. His fine collection is open to the public. Details of opening times can be obtained from the National Council for the Conservation of Plants and Gardens (NCCPG) Directory.

If you need detailed information about the taxonomy and nomenclature of euphorbias, the best place to start looking for information is the *World Checklist and Bibliography of Euphorbiaceae* Volume 2 (ISBN 1-9003-4784-9). This was published by the Royal Botanic Gardens Kew in 2000 and compiled by Raphaël Govaerts, David G. Frodin and Alan Radcliffe-Smith.

INDEX

Page numbers in **bold** refer
to illustrations

ACKNOWLEDGEMENTS

Illustrations: Patrick Mulrey
Copy-editor: Simon Maughan
RHS Editor: Barbara Haynes
Proofreader: Rae Spencer-Jones
Index: Dorothy Frame

The Publisher would like to thank
the following people for their kind
permission to reproduce their
photographs:

The Garden Picture Library: 7 (Howard
Rice).

Timothy Walker (all other pages).

Those pictures on pages 35, 37, 59 and
91 were taken at Hadspen House ©
Sandra and Nori Pope.

Jacket Image: Garden Picture Library
(Jerry Pavia).